India

OTHER BOOKS ABOUT MAJOR CULTURES OF THE WORLD

Land of the Pharaohs, by Leonard Cottrell

Maya: Land of the Turkey and the Deer, by Victor W. von Hagen

The Chinese Way of Life, by Lin Yutang

The Byzantines, by Thomas Caldecot Chubb

The Arabs, by Harry B. Ellis

The Sun Kingdom of the Aztecs, by Victor W. von Hagen

India

by WALTER A. FAIRSERVIS, Jr.

ILLUSTRATED BY *Richard M. Powers*

THE WORLD PUBLISHING COMPANY

CLEVELAND AND NEW YORK

Published by The World Publishing Company
2231 West 110th Street, Cleveland 2, Ohio

Published simultaneously in Canada by
Nelson, Foster & Scott Ltd.

Library of Congress Catalog Card Number: 61-9087

The selections on pages 74, 84, 85, and 88–89 from A. L. Basham's
The Wonder That Was India, are used by permission of The Macmillan Company
and Sidgwick and Jackson, Ltd.

To the memory of
Alice V. Brower and Mary H. Riddle,
teachers extraordinary

Contents

India

The Fascination of India

Alexander of Macedon was the greatest conqueror on the earth. More than three hundred years before Christ, he led his army across the known world, subjugating all the city states, the kingdoms, and the empires from Greece to the gates of India in less than eight years. Tall, powerfully built, handsome as Apollo, and victor in a hundred battles, Alexander was a superior man. "A god," many thought him: "The son of Zeus the Almighty"; and Alexander of the Silver Helmet, whose ancient shield of Achilles had caught the arrows of doomed Troy, might well have thought himself a god. For everything was his: Athens the Golden, the Marbled Isles of the Aegean, Phoenician Tyre, mysterious Egypt and the great desert beyond the Nile, Babylon of the Mighty Walls, all the vast lands that circled the Salt Desert where the smoking ruins of imperial Persia marked his path. Everything was his, even the grass steppe that led to the rim of the world and the snow-capped mountains of the dawn. Yes, everything, except this land of Hind that we call India, which stretched in heat-shimmered brown hills eastward beyond his sight.

For the first time Alexander felt the pangs of doubt. He had set out to conquer the whole world, but there seemed to be no end to it. Where were the bounds of India? "Beyond . . . beyond," he was told at the edge of each river and the top of each hill. Always "beyond," until finally his troops would go no farther. They had faced the savage hordes of Scythia, the fierce horsemen of Bactria, and the scythed chariots of Persian Darius. Even the war elephants of King Porus had not daunted them. But this never-ending "beyond" and this hot world of white-garbed brown men, who celebrated mysterious rites in the worship of strange gods and knew nothing of the Mediterranean world, were something they could no longer face. No amount of pleading or threatening could change their minds, and so at last Alexander had to turn back.

But the world-conqueror wanted to know more about India before he left. How far had he really come on his way to the bounds of the earth? He was told of some wise men living near-by whose wisdom was famous throughout India. "Bring them to me," he commanded an officer.

The messenger found the wise men sitting on a rock. Naked,

they sat, and cross-legged, ignoring the heat, the flies, and their own hunger.

"Come, Alexander wants to see you!" commanded the officer.

"Why should we come?" answered the spokesman for the ascetics.

"Because Alexander, son of Zeus, commands it."

"Alexander is no more the son of Zeus than I am. For if God be Zeus and men are sons of God, then we as men are both sons of Zeus."

"If you come, Alexander will not hurt you. He will give you gifts if you will serve him."

"What can your Alexander give to wise men? For all he has are earthly riches, and true wisdom is above all earthly things."

Exasperated, the officer said, "If you do not come at once, Alexander will have you killed!"

With a smile the wise man answered, "Then I would thank him for freeing my soul from its prison of flesh."

When the officer returned and told these things to the restless conqueror, Alexander commented, "What a land is this!" and turned half sadly to the preparations for departure.

Alexander's feelings about India have been shared by many men. They have been drawn by its wealth, its faith, its vastness; they have been repelled by its heat, its diseases, its human miseries. But for all, there has been a fascination which gives India a peculiar place in the thoughts of men.

What is this fascination? Even if we wrote a hundred volumes instead of one, we could never encompass more than a tiny fraction of the reasons India has played such an important role in human history. Yet we should try, for even a small glimpse of the true India is worth a great deal.

First of all, there is the land itself. Extending in a great

wedge shape from the southern border of the highest mountains in the world to within a few degrees of the equator, its geography makes it a land of contrasts. One remembers these contrasts as a series of varied pictures: coconut palms hanging over salt-water lagoons near Madras, enormous expanses of reed marshes at the mouth of the Ganges River at Calcutta, the arid desert coast which ships follow to Karachi. Inland are forested valleys and grassy hills which are the seats of the fabulous kingdoms of Mysore and Hyderabad. The Ganges flows through a flat land of endlessly tilled fields where, here and there, patches or ribbons of trees and bushes mark the course of a river or canal; while the mighty Indus River winds like the Nile between deserts of desolation to bring life to the people of Sind. Dense jungles spill from the foothills of the Himalayas, almost blocking the road to Nepal. Kashmir is a land of pines and lakes in whose waters are mirrored the snow-capped mountains that surround the vale and the marble palaces of Moghul emperors. And at last one comes to the stern barren mountains of the northwest frontier in whose valleys Pathan villagers guard stone villages or watch the caravans along the Khyber Pass; then the mighty ranges of Hindu Kush, Karakorum, or the Himalayas in whose midst the towering peaks of Everest, Kanchenjunga, and Godwin Austen mark the roof of the world, the great barriers that isolate India from the rest of Asia.

The land and its climate are inseparable, and it is the climate of India that shapes the character of man and land alike. Except in high Kashmir and the mountain lands, heat is the ruling force in India. A seemingly endless, all-pervading, baking heat that distorts the air with dust devils and shimmering waves. Turbans, draped robes, naked feet, dark skins; thick-walled houses, open-mesh beds, fans in the ceiling, balconies, porches; fantastic networks of canals, ditches and channels, fountains, pools; hours of labor, hours of rest, outlook on the world; will, desire, ambition, hope, fear and love; on and on and on, innumerable are the things that heat has caused the men who live in India to do, to think, and to dream. Jacobabad in western Pakistan is the hot-center of the world, averaging 97° Fahrenheit each year. New Delhi, capital of modern India, frequently registers 112° in the shade in summer.

But just when the heat, which has intensified from March to May, has reached a stage when it seems that life itself must burn away, great dark clouds fill the sky in the southwest, the desultory wind rises to a gale. The sun, till now glimpsed as a red orb in a brown-white haze, disappears behind the monster clouds and with a crash of angry thunder and seering lightning the rains pour earthward, not in "sheets" or "buckets" but by seas and oceans. For three months much of India receives this rain. In the Khasi Hills of the northeast the rainfall may be over 400 inches a year, while at Delhi and Lahore it may be 25 inches. Western India, on the other hand, may have only a few inches of moisture during the summer months, but here water eventually comes from the mountains along the river beds. The Punjab in western India is called the Land of Five Rivers, and is one of the most flourishing regions of all India.

During the hot months of the spring and summer many people go to hill stations where the air is as cool as temperate climate anywhere. These are delightful places of bubbling streams, bright flowers, and spectacular scenery. However, during the wintertime the wind comes whistling out of central Asia through the valleys of Tibet, bringing cold weather and snow to the hills and moderating the climate of the plains. For the people of India the wintertime generally is a good time.

But who are these people? One anthropologist has commented that almost every race in the Old World except the Negro has lived in India at one time or another. When the British ruled India they soon discovered that not only were there many races, but that the tribal, language, caste, and cultural differences within these races were enormous. All these differences were created by the dynamic movement of peoples and cultures filtering from one place to another, mixing words, inventions, ideas, and bloodlines. For example, Alexander stayed hardly a year in western India, but he started something that was to leave a permanent mark on a large part of the country.

Alexander's garrisons stayed on as rulers in his name in Afghanistan and the hills bordering the Indus River. After his death the descendants of his soldiers created an empire which lasted in one form or another for over three hundred years. In the hill country the Pathans, the tribes who live near the Khyber Pass, still speak of Iskander the Great, and the number of fair-haired, blue- or hazel-eyed people among them leaves little doubt that the Greeks were indeed resident there. In the far valleys of the Karakorum there still survive rites of ritual plowing that remind one of the annual festivals of Demeter and of Dionysus celebrated in Greece before the Age of Pericles. Most remarkable of all is to see the images of Buddha dressed in Greek or Roman clothing and appearing before the world with the face of Apollo or Hermes. The curls of hair that roll over the forehead might well have graced the brow of Alexander himself!

But the Greeks were of minor importance in shaping the character of India. They were but one drop in the flood of people who came to the subcontinent. First, there were probably the Stone Age hunters like those of Java and China. These primitive men have left their tools on the banks of the Indus, the Ganges, and the Narbada. Then came a short, dark-skinned, broad-nosed, long-armed race who spoke a tongue called Dravidian. Today, their home is in the hills of southern India, but once they were probably found all over the subcontinent. Then after 3000 B.C. the Mediterranean peoples of the Near East moved across the Iranian Plateau and slowly drove them out.

This tall, slender, brown-skinned race quickly inhabited northern India, and the Dravidians were probably forced deeper into the forests. The Mediterranean people seem to have brought agriculture and to have carried it over India. Whatever language they first spoke, some of them picked up Dravidian, especially those who moved south. Lots of them must have married Dravidians, for their races merged.

Around 1200 B.C. the great cities the Mediterranean people had built in the Indus Valley were destroyed by a group of nomads from central Asia. Calling themselves Aryans, they came as conquerors, but they remained as residents and settled into the pattern of India. Yet the newcomers brought changes; they developed modern Hinduism and created a class system which was to stratify Indian daily life around religion. They too added their culture and blood to the older India.

Later a bewildering number of invaders perpetuated the mixture of India's cultures and peoples. Scythians, Persians, Huns, Turks, Burmese, Siamese, Tibetans, Arabs, Malays, even Portuguese, Dutch, French, and British crossed the barriers of sea and mountain to conquer, loot, reside, and be absorbed. One dominated for a while and then the other, and each culture left a trace of itself somewhere. It might be an architectural motif, an art form, a new language, a new religion. Whatever its quality, each left a mark.

But we have spoken of the fascination of India. Again we must think in terms of pictures. We cannot visualize 400 million people or over thirty languages, both of which are vital facts about Indians. But we can see the tall bearded Sikh, the short green-clothed Gurkha, the slender dark-skinned Bengali, the bushy-headed Toda, the aristocratic Rajput, the proud Pathan. We can find names of India's most famous men, like Akbar, Harsha, Kalidasa, Gandhi, Buddha, and Nehru, and in their records see the kind of humanity that exists in the tiniest child surviving in the cauldron of India. For part of the lure of India is its tremendous vitality. This quality is found in every aspect of Indian life, in the extremes of poverty and riches, of dirt and cleanliness, of light humor and profound philosophy, of primitivism and great technical advancement, the jeweled rajah and the filthy begger, the motor car and the elephant, the new paved street and the sacred cow walking along it.

But another part of the lure is the sense of history in the making. India is a land of high adventure. During the rule of the British in the eighteenth and nineteenth centuries, young Englishmen, drawn to adventure, volunteered to cross the seas and serve in India for years in the service of the Crown just for the chance of adventure. And no wonder, for there were places to see, wars to fight, animals to hunt, and honor to be won. The children of Sussex, Devon, or London could sleep with mighty dreams of romance conjured up by names like Bengal, the Khyber Pass, Delhi, Oudh, Kabul, Benares, and Lucknow. Visions of the Taj Mahal and the fairy palaces of Kashmir, of elephants at Jaipur and the jewels of Hind, rose in their minds. Who would not have given his life to hunt the tiger or face King Cobra, or sail through phosphorescent seas past Adam's Peak to the roads of Calcutta, or gallop full tilt at the foe in the battle garb of a Bengal Lancer! Here was color and duty, danger and romance, that only India could offer.

Poets like Wordsworth and writers like Kipling and Thackeray, generals like Napoleon and Alexander, sailors like da Gama and Columbus, all grew up dreaming of India and were haunted by their visions of it. Visions that made some of them travel far from home and security, and by so doing, help to change the world.

I have written of these things because as we look at India on the following pages we must remember that the real India and the India of men's dreams are never far apart. To know its splendor you must know its poverty, to know its importance you must know its history and its culture. Above all, remember that India has many sides, and like the thousand arms of the Hindu god Siva, each has a meaning.

A Land of Villages

India is a land of villages. It is said that between the Plateau of Iran and the Bay of Bengal there are over 700,000 villages containing more than 350 million people!

India has great cities too, and names like Delhi, Bombay, Karachi, and Calcutta are familiar to all of us. The cities of India are of three kinds. First there are the old fortified cities like Delhi, Hyderabad, and Gwalior. Some of these are surrounded by massive walls topped with towers and pierced by pinnacled gates; others have magnificent citadels crowning heights that overlook the plain on which the city is built. Such cities reflect the long centuries of wars which plagued India as they did the rest of the world.

Then there are the port cities famous in recent history as the sea-gates of India: Karachi on the Arabian Sea is the chief port of West Pakistan, the Moslem state of the Indian subcontinent; Calcutta, Madras, and Bombay were the port cities founded by the British East India Company in the seventeenth century. These have grown to be the largest cities of India, seats of vast commercial activities and chief ports of call for the ships of the world.

Probably the most characteristically Indian cities are those which Indians regard as holy. Undoubtedly the most famous of these is Benares. Indeed, for the Hindus, Benares is as important to their faith as Jerusalem is to the Christians or

Mecca to the Moslems. Every year pilgrims come there to worship in some of the many temples that crowd the city. But the chief attraction are the ghats, platforms built along the shore of the Ganges where the people cremate their dead and bathe in the water.

The Ganges is the most sacred river in a land where many rivers—like the Godavari, Indus, and Brahmaputra—are regarded as holy. Some believe that the Ganges springs from the topknot of the Hindu god Siva and he whose ashes are thrown into the stream passes to salvation. The Ganges cleanses from the living all sins and bad actions.

Each Hindu tries to reach Benares at some time in his life. Beggars come to receive alms from the faithful, who by charity seek to acquire good from the gods; learned men find Benares a center of learning, and even Westerners come to the colleges and universities to be taught ancient philosophies and living religions. Benares is a crowded city, teeming with activities— not all of them sacred. As in many Indian cities, crafts of many kinds are carried on, with the products being sold in bazaars. Benares is famous for its fine silk and gold brocade, brassware, and incense. These are some of the things that drew Europeans to India; and these local industries, together with the wealth brought by pilgrims, have made this city one of the most flourishing. What a wonderful place it is with its countless temples, painted buildings, carved porches and balconies, and its ever-varied population representing all India.

But whereas the importance of the cities has fluctuated during their history, India's villages have always remained as the homes of most of her people, and as such, have never varied a jot in importance no matter what the events of history.

An Indian village is merely a cluster of houses usually near a source of water. The kind of house varies with the region. In

Bengal on the east, the house might be a rectangular building with walls of bamboo and a peaked roof of thatch; in Sind on the west, it might be a square house of mud brick with a flat adobe roof; while down in Travancore in the far south, it would not be unusual to see a house made of branches standing high on stilts.

But no matter where the village is located and no matter with what material the houses are made, there are certain characteristics which all the villages seem to share. There is usually a main street to which all paths lead. On this might be located the village school, a meeting hall or tea shop serving the same purpose, a dispensary and a post office—if the village is large enough to have some or all of these things. People with things to sell bring them here and display them; if there are several vendors gathered there, it becomes a bazaar or shopping center. Some of the more well-to-do villagers may have their homes on the main village street, and certain it is that easy access can be had from here to the home of the village headman or chief.

Main Street in India has almost the same function as in the United States: it is the center of activity, the place where people get together for trade, talk, or celebration. Even the village barber is there, but in India both the barber and his customers squat on the ground, so the barber may be found anywhere along the street where there is a patch of shade.

Another characteristic feature is the village well or pool. This is the main source of water, and since it is the function of women to fetch water for the house, to bathe the children, and to wash clothes, women's lives outside the home center around the village wells and pools. This is the best place to hear village gossip. It is also the most colorful place in the village, for while the men of India usually wear plain white clothes—

generally a dhoti, a kind of wrap around—the women do quite the opposite. They dress themselves in wonderful colors and jewelry, even though they are just going to the well. Even the poorest women wear the graceful sari or a full dhoti and join their more well-to-do sisters in piercing ears and noses in

order to hang colorful ornaments there. In addition there are forehead ornaments, finger rings, toe rings, anklets, necklaces, chest ornaments, hairpins, and dozens of bangles for the arms. Every imaginable material is used for this jewelry: gold, silver, copper, nickel, steel, tin, brass, zinc, glass, turquoise, flint, enamel, sea shells, even bits of mirror. Of course, it isn't always easy to see this finery, especially if you are a man, for among the Moslems a woman usually observes purdah outside her home. That is, she must conceal her face and form from every eye. To do this she sometimes wears the burka, a veil which covers her completely, and she can only see the world through the holes in an embroidered panel set in her veil. In her everyday work at home, however, she uses only a wisp of a cloth over the top of her head as do the Hindus who do not observe purdah.

There is always at least one holy place in or near the village. The Moslems have a mosque, while the Hindus have shrines. The Hindu shrines may be found anywhere in the village, but frequently they are placed near a pool of water and in the shade of trees. Water plays a very important part in both Hindu and Moslem ceremonies. It is necessary to purify oneself by washing or bathing before praying to the gods, and so having a pool of water close by is very convenient. But it also makes the setting for worship rather fine. The view of a shrine or temple amid trees by quiet waters is one of the loveliest sights in India.

Throughout this book one has to consider that the Indian subcontinent is a land of religions. People are generally classified in Indian census-taking by their faiths. There are Christians, Buddhists, and Parsees, the latter worshipers of Zoroastrianism, the faith of ancient Persia. Then there are the Jains, followers of the teachings of Mahavira, one of the early saints of India. There are even animists, those who personify rocks, animals, plants, and the like. Most of these live in the jungle areas. The two major religions are Hinduism and Islam, the Moslem religion founded by Mohammed.

The Mohammedan faith was brought to India by the Arabs in the centuries following 800 A.D. It is now the faith of about 70 million people, most of whom live in Pakistan, the Moslem state created when the British left in 1947. The basic population of India is Hindu. Hinduism is therefore one of the world's greatest religions, since it is followed by over 300 million people. It is the state religion of modern India, and when we speak of the Hindus we mean those who are adherents of Hinduism. But when we speak of Indians, we could mean Moslems, Parsees, or Jains as well. That is why we have to make religious distinctions now and again when speaking of India. For a village may contain people of several faiths all living together, identical in every way except in religious features.

Practically all villages, except those of the nomad and the fisherman, are located in the midst of cultivated fields. More than any other occupation, Indians are farmers. The plowing of the earth and the planting, tilling, and harvesting of crops occupy them practically all their lives. Therefore it is only natural that their villages are set right in the middle of the fields, convenient to their daily labor. And it is good that the getting to the fields is not very difficult, for these farmers live a hard and demanding life. In much of India the months from March through May are the summer months. Then daily temperatures rise very high, the mean being 100° and over in many places. The fields become hard-baked, so hard in fact that they look like flat plains of brown rock. The roads and paths are dusty lanes along which men and animals are veiled by tawny clouds rising at every step. Only here and there where water still remains in storage pools, called *tanks,* or where trees are carefully nurtured, is the scene relieved by a bit of green color. It is a time when human energy is at its lowest, sapped by the all-pervading heat.

But along about late May a few light showers fall, enough to soften the ground. It is then that the farmer hitches his bullocks or oxen (if he has either) to his wooden plow and sets to work. He does not mind working in the rain, for it is not only cooling but it keeps the ground soft for his plow. Sticky though the muddy earth is, it cannot help but feel good as it oozes over his feet and around his ankles.

This is just about the right time of year for the planting of house gardens, which are the main sources of vegetables. Indians like okra, onions, pumpkins, beans, and various kinds of gourds. These vegetables are particularly susceptible to insect pests and droughts, so many Hindus consult with the Brahman priest in order to discover what the best day for planting might be. The Brahman checks the stars and sets a date, and the farmer follows his advice scrupulously.

But the most important food crops are millet, corn, and rice; and as soon as the rains are steady enough, along about June, these crops are sown.

These rains are called *monsoons,* and in much of India they arrive suddenly and dramatically and always when the weather seems to be most unbearable. The air feels as thick and heavy as syrup—and just as hard to breathe—and the heat is so fierce that to walk ten feet seems to require all one's will power. But then on the horizon to the southwest enormous blackish clouds appear, rising rapidly higher and coming ever nearer, assuming fantastic forms as they gradually fill the sky. Now they look like great woolly blankets, then they are herds of camels, then monster elephants, and at last enormous arms reaching out of shapeless monsters. A scuttling sound, and the leaves of the great banyan tree begin to tremble, and the spade-shaped leaves of the fig start to sway. A breeze, growing in force, sweeps dust along the streets and into the houses. To sweat-coated faces it feels like something beyond mere pleasure, like the first bite of a fresh peach or the morning of the first snow. Now the white angry sun is blotted out; there is nothing but a gray darkness in which swaying trees and running people proclaim an excited world. Then come steely flashes of lightning and constant deep-throated thunder so prolonged that even the barking dogs sound like mere crickets in the night. At long, long last, with a burst and a roar, the rain crashes down. At first the too dry, powdery earth puffs from the impact; but in no time at all it becomes sleek and shiny and one becomes aware that it has a good smell which had almost been forgotten in the long hot months just past.

The Hindus have a festival that they celebrate in June. It is to worship the preserver god, Vishnu. It is no wonder that a celebration for the preserver is held at such a time—at the coming of the monsoon—for the rains bring life to India. Though the thatched roofs leak and the streets turn to mud, the crops are assured of life-giving moisture, and the village will survive for another year.

By November the fields are harvested and are almost immediately replanted with winter crops such as castor beans, mustard, chilis, garlic, onions, and coriander, most of which are used to give the characteristic hot taste to Indian food. The winter crops are irrigated by water from the village storage tank which may have been dug hundreds of years before. During this period the air is filled with sounds: the yell of the farmer as he drives his bullocks, "Ayyyyahhhh"; the regular *clit-clit, clat-clat* of the Persian water wheel as water is raised from wells for the onion crop; and the chatter of women near-by as they walk tall and straight along the paths, carrying pots of water on their heads. (It sounds like a flock of soft-tongued birds with now and then a grackle thrown in!)

A village is much more than just a cluster of houses in the midst of fields, however. A village really is the symbol of the Indian way of life. It is a place for people to be born, to be brought up, to marry, to have children, to work, and to die—all in a characteristically Indian way. Indians take pride in their villages and they love the land and the things about them. The first time I was in an Indian village I saw a man off by himself, crying, and was told that he had just sold a cow.

"But why should that make him cry?"

"Because the cow was one with his family. It is like selling his own son."

But walk into a village; the first thing that attracts your attention will be a dog or rather several dogs. In the hill villages of Baluchistan or the old Northwest Frontier, these dogs are big, fierce, deep-chested fellows with tails and ears cropped for combat; but down on the alluvial plains of the Indus, the Ganges, and the Narbada they are yappy brown dogs with bony tails and lots of ribs showing. The noise they make is stupendous and tells the villagers someone is coming. A stone tossed in the dogs' direction holds them off; they have been hit too many times before, poor fellows, to take a chance of being hit again.

Now something else holds your senses. It is the pungent smell of cow dung, for the basic fuel of India is a cake made of cow manure and straw mixed with water and dried in the sun. There is no better fuel, for wood, coal, and kerosene are virtually unobtainable.

For the Westerner and for many Indians, too, there are things which are disturbing but can't be ignored. Flies every-where—on the ears and snouts of the bullocks, in the eyes of children, on cooked rice standing in the sun, on that rain puddle in the middle of street—everywhere. There are few latrines in village India, and people use their fields instead. It is good for the crops, but terrible for human life. And too often one sees people with blinded eyes, and animals and humans with open sores, both the result of poor nutrition and terrible sanitation. During the year round, one hears the wailing of women at the death of a loved one more often than not. But it is important to know these things, for it helps make under-standable so much of Indian life. A life that is bound to the village, which is its source of living and at the same time the cause of its death. This is the Indian paradox, a paradox that lies at the very heart of village religion.

In the village street there are many things to catch one's eye: carved wooden posts by a door; a gaily painted plastered wall; the deep shade of a thatched roof-overhang; the serpen-tine folds of the massive banyan tree; the rich greens of the mango; a woman slapping dough on a stone; an old bearded man in the shadows of a porch; a warm brown cow, with a hump and soft liquid eyes, walking unrestrained along the street. A couple of young men are having an argument, and the sound of their voices rasps shrilly in the air. They spit betel-nut juice in red jets on the ground as they wave their arms about to emphasize a point. A few people gather and one or two elders shake their heads. "It is never good to lose one's balance. Arguments lead to quarrels, and quarrels pre-vent the doing of things in the right way," goes the saying. The argument calms in a moment, and the young men look about somewhat shamefaced.

One enters the house of a more well-to-do family through a gate in a mud wall opening into a courtyard. The house itself is on the opposite side of the yard. On the right is the cattle barn with a place for storing cakes of cattle-dung fuel. A fine mango tree usually grows in one corner of the yard and acts as a shade tree for one end of the porch of the main house. The porch is a raised platform of mud brick in which wooden pillars are set to hold up a sloping roof of thatch. A really wealthy person might even have a tile roof. This porch is the family social area, and in the summer the whole family sleeps here. On one side of the porch is a bed, called a *charpoy*. It is a wooden frame on four legs, with a net of cord or reed woven across it. A good charpoy is very comfortable because it is broad and long and its open mesh permits good circulation of air from the underside—ideal for hot weather.

The mud walls of the house are very thick, which is also very good in summer. In northwestern India, especially in arid regions like Sind and Baluchistan, shafts connected to ventilator scoops on the roof are placed in the walls. These scoops catch the prevailing wind and bring air down into the house. Sometimes a net of wet branches is placed over the inside opening, and this may lower the temperature as much as fifteen degrees. It is the earliest air-conditioner.

Inside the house is another courtyard with a deep basin where ladies can bathe. Doorways around the sides of the court lead into a variety of rooms: storerooms, sleeping rooms, a dining room, and of course the kitchen. Since this is a house for prosperous people, practically all the walls are white-washed and some are decorated with drawings of local design and even human and animal figures.

If one is a guest, he probably eats with the family on the front porch. A member of the family might as easily eat in the dining room. Even though this family is wealthy by village standards, there is very little furniture. Several wooden benches, a couple of stools, and perhaps a table. But these people take pride in their pots and pans, especially the metal ones which are usually kept very shiny. Another obvious article of importance is the large pottery water jug placed in the corner of rooms.

But above all one is aware of how well swept everything is. The sweeper women with their bundle-of-branches brooms keep the mud floors scrupulously clean of particles, and so when one sits down on the reed mats on the floor there is certain to be a clean surface beneath. Among the Moslems of the West, cushions and carpets are required features of the living quarters, but among the Hindus these are not so common. In fact in most Indian villages reed mats are generally a luxury.

Now food is brought. This is a critical time for Indians. First of all, both Moslems and higher caste Hindus wash before eating. I remember in a Pathan village near the Khyber Pass politely washing my hands while a servant poured water over them from a long spouted brass ewer, while over his shoulder he supported a clean towel for my use. My Moslem friends who followed me not only washed their hands, but with great gusto and the rhythmic accompaniment of grunts, groans, and gargles scrubbed their faces, necks, and swished out their mouths while the towel and servant got wetter and wetter!

Only the men assemble on the floor, for generally women are excluded and must wait until the men have finished. Among some households the young men must wait until the elders have completed their meal before eating: this is a traditional mark of respect among both Hindus and Moslems.

Indian villagers eat with their hands. There is an unleavened cake or bread called *chappatti* or *paratha*. Flat in shape, it is torn into convenient pieces with which to grasp the hot curried rice and the chunks of meat that a host may offer his guests if he can afford it. The chili peppers and curry burn Western throats, but tea, bananas, and a wonderful cool pudding called *khir* cool one's mouth afterward. Here again the bulk of the villagers don't have all these things. A little millet gruel, a few handfuls of rice, and some chili powder make a daily diet for millions of people who count themselves fortunate to have so much!

Then, too, there are religious differences that prevent the eating of certain foods by some groups. For instance, the Moslems have sanctions against eating pork as do the Hindus against beef. In fact, the Brahmans, or priest class, won't eat any meat at all.

This whole matter of eating is regarded by the people of India as more than just a means of staying alive. It has very serious and profound significance, especially among the Hindus. It doesn't take long to realize that the people of the villages are classified by one another not only by the kind of daily labor each performs, or by their wealth or lack of it, but also by their social status. Traditionally the Brahmans can never accept food from someone in a lower status than themselves, and so Brahmans have to serve Brahmans. On the other hand, practically everybody will eat food prepared by Brahmans, because they are regarded as pure and holy. But there are groups with whom nobody can eat or accept their food. These people are considered the lowest of the low and are sometimes called the *untouchables;* their status has been one that is slowly improving in Hindu India.

Between the untouchables and the Brahmans village society

is divided up into units, called *castes,* which center around one
or another occupation. These castes are classified as equal,
higher, or lower, according to one's own status. For example,
traders are generally classified higher than farmers. Potters
and shepherds are the equal of some farmers and higher than
others. Weavers and barbers are lower than the farmers but
higher than the hunters, and so on. Usually everyone will
gladly accept food from one of a higher or equal caste but not
from one that is lower. Nowadays, however, there are certain
kinds of food acceptable whether offered from below or above
one's social status.

No one may marry anyone outside his or her own caste. In
fact, Hindu marriage arrangements are very complicated. A
boy doesn't simply fall in love with a girl and then marry her.
His caste has very strict rules about whom he can marry. Each
caste has a number of divisions, and the boy cannot go outside his division to chose his marital partner. But this is only
the beginning of the matter, because each division is further
divided into units called *gotrams,* and a boy has to marry a
girl outside his own gotram. Gotrams, in turn, are divided into
smaller units called *vanshams,* which are almost like families.
They are really joint families, and everyone in them regards
his fellow vanshamite as a brother or sister, even though they
are not related by blood. Naturally, it is forbidden to marry
someone in one's own vansham, since that would be like
marrying one's own brother or sister. If a member of the vansham dies, he or she is mourned just as if he were someone in
one's own family.

Complicated as these social matters may seem, they really
work very well and insure the continuance of the efficient village way of life. Though the different castes may not associate
with each other in many ways, they are none the less depen-

dent on one another. Whole families of untouchables may attach themselves to a farming family and work in the fields as laborers. In return for this work, they get food and cloth. These families may have worked together for generations, just as the farmer's barber may cut the farmer's hair every month in the same way that the barber's father cut the hair of the farmer's father before him, and his grandfather before that. This interdependence of castes in Hindu villages functions throughout the year in all kinds of activities and occasions: birth, death, marriage, religious ceremonies, and visits by outsiders. During such critical seasons as the time for planting and the time for harvesting, the village would be in serious trouble if the castes didn't work together. It is very likely that

this was the reason the caste system got started in the first place.

You will probably read or hear from others, especially Westerners, about how really bad the caste system is because it keeps everyone in his place and makes him unable to take advantage of opportunities to better himself. Certainly there are bad things about the system, such as the poor lot of the lowest castes, but for the hard life of the Indian village there can be no question but that castes have done many good things. In any case, the caste system is very much an Indian way of life. It has deeply affected even non-Hindu groups like the Moslems, who don't have castes but still like to classify people by occupations so that one is inferior or superior according to what one does.

Of course caste members would never think of doing the jobs performed by another caste. There is an ancient saying: "It is better to do one's own duty badly than another's well."

Many castes proclaim their activities by carrying about the tools of their trade as if they were the banners of knighthood. Barbers snap their scissors noisily; smiths whip their hammers in the air with fine, full motions; the hunters display their

game, which usually consists of a sorry hare or a few small birds, as if they had trapped an imperial elk. One has to see to appreciate the costumes and equipment of the men and women of the castes that provide entertainment, itinerant services, or roadside barter. Acrobats, magicians, storytellers, snake charmers, actors, and musicians roam the dusty roads of India dressed in all kinds of colorful clothes, carrying the tools of their trades. For a few annas, they are ready to provide a wealth of entertainment—entertainment that in form, at least, has been unchanged for thousands of years. So far do these people roam that their visits to each village are only occasional, but they do contribute by breaking up the monotony of village life.

There are other times when village families break away from their daily labors and have fun. One of these is when a wedding takes place. A good friend of mine, Gupta Das, invited me to his wedding in his native village, and even though he had been away from home studying in Delhi, the wedding was celebrated exactly as if he had been working on the farm every day.

Gupta Das's future wife was from a neighboring village. His parents had arranged the marriage with her parents, and neither of the young couple had had anything to do with it. Of course I'm speaking technically, for my friend Das had been at a friend's house in that village on many occasions before he had gone to the city. And since his friend happened to be the brother of the girl he was about to marry, I'm quite sure the young couple had glimpsed one another on more than one occasion. Then, too, Das's sister had sometimes visited at the future bride's house, and certainly a lot of questions had been answered then.

Gupta Das and Ajanti, the bride, were to be married during

the days following the Hindu festival of Chauti, which occurs in August every year. The days had been picked by the Brahman as being especially auspicious for their wedding because they were sacred to the god Ganesha. Ganesha is an elephant god whose images were all over the village when we arrived. Flowers and leaf dishes containing rice had been placed before each image, and ritual markings in vermilion and yellow could be seen on Ganesha's forehead and trunk. It is said that he who worships Ganesha during the festival of Chauti will have his wishes come true, so certainly it is an ideal time to have a wedding.

One would have thought that all would be happy during Chauti, but when we first arrived in the village street the noise of angry shouts and abusive language was everywhere. It seemed that really no one was happy. That is, until we noticed that some of the people who were being shouted at were smiling.

"Why are these people smiling when they are being shouted at?"

"Because they have seen the moon."

"The moon?"

"Yes, it's very unlucky to see the moon during Chauti."

"Why?"

"Because if you do, you will be falsely accused of stealing something during the year."

"Yes, but why all the shouting?"

"The ones who are being shouted at have seen the moon during Chauti, and since it is believed that their ill luck can only be taken away if someone abuses them, they make some mischief so that people will be angry at them and will shout at them!"

This incident is a good example of the apparent contradictions in Indian life that are so difficult for a Westerner to understand.

The next day Gupta Das and his entire family, as well as his friends, set out for Ajanti's village some three miles away. Everyone had on his best clothes, and Gupta Das was especially handsome in a fresh white dhoti and shirt, with a flower garland hanging over his shoulders. Everyone in Ajanti's village was out to greet us. Her family was of upper-caste status and her father quite prosperous, so this wedding was a little more elaborate than usual.

There was a separate house for us to stay in, swept clean and complete with clean cloth, mats, pottery, and fresh flowers everywhere. There was no question that the groom's family got a favorable impression of their future daughter-in-law's family. Gupta Das's mother was especially observant and it was well she was pleased, because she could have easily stopped the wedding if she had wished.

Dinner was really a feast held at the bride's house. Every possible good thing had been brought for our satisfaction. Even cashew nuts, oranges, and figs had been purchased for the occasion. A mountain of curried rice, rich with great chunks of mutton and lentils, was the main course and our shining brass plates were practically buried beneath the food. The last dish was a delicate white pudding covered with fine silver paper and decorated with deep green leaves. We ate everything together—paper and all!

Of course everyone was anxious to see the bride, but she never appeared, though Gupta Das's sister and mother visited with her for a while.

Early the next day we were visited by the bride's sisters and mother, who brought us water to wash with and some tooth-picklike sticks "to clean our mouths." This was the day of the wedding, and after breakfast Gupta Das at last joined his bride. The two knelt before the shrine of the family god and performed a little ritual of worship. For the groom, among other things, it meant his recognition of his wife's piety and his intention to wed her in full acknowledgment of the powers of life and the creation of life which the gods give marriage. For the bride this was the first real joining of herself to her husband which she acknowledges before the god of her family.

The Brahman had appointed four o'clock that afternoon for the major ceremonies. Just before that time the bride's family escorted the bridegroom and guests to a kind of pavilion set up in the compound of the bride's home. Flowers were everywhere—in garlands, in bunches, and in the hair of all the ladies. The floor was covered with fine mats and a carpet or two. There was a sacred fire burning in a brazier, and near it stood the Brahman, looking very solemn in his white robes. We arrived in a gay procession and sat in a circle around the kneeling bride and groom. It was just four o'clock when the Brahman began to chant religious verses. I noticed that some joined in and in the midst of this, Gupta Das and Ajanti repeated their marriage vows which pledged them to support one another as long as they lived. Then he placed a fine necklace of delicate black beads around her neck and tied it in place. This necklace is a kind of wedding ring which proclaims to everyone that Ajanti is a married woman. Gupta then put a fine silver ring on each of Ajanti's second toes.

The two rose and went to the fire. There, they sat side by side while incense was thrown into the fire, sending a deep pungent smell throughout the pavilion. The Brahman continued to chant, and all was very solemn but certainly very beautiful. Ajanti was dressed in a saffron-yellow sari with a gossamer veil over her head. A fine silver ornament hung from

her hair over her forehead, and her lower eyelids were del-
icately shaded with blue-green kohl. Her ears were almost
covered with great silver shell earrings while her arms and
hands, at which she continued to gaze in proper modesty,
were bright with silver and gold bangles and rings. I heard
later that it had taken three full days to prepare her for the
wedding. Days in which she was ritually bathed, combed, and
fed by her womanfolk. The smoke of the incense, the bright
costumes, flowers, and bits of colored paper and cloth which
hung here and there made a wonderful scene.

That night there was a real celebration: food for everyone,
songs, and much laughter. But the bride and groom still had to
behave with formality. They were seated facing one another,
and around them on the floor were designs drawn with various colors of rice paste. This area separated them from the
rest of us, and in so doing gave them very great importance,
which was only right of course. Then Gupta Das did a strange
thing. He suddenly took a small ball of rice from his plate and
tossed it into Ajanti's plate. Immediately the whole place became silent. Ajanti seemed to hesitate, so Gupta Das did it
again. Still she hesitated. He waited a moment and then tossed
a third ball into her plate. This time, with the utmost delicacy,
Ajanti took a little lump of rice from her own bowl and tossed
it into the plate of her husband. A sigh went around the room,
and with a burst of noise the feast went on. After that the
tossing of the food was almost a secret game between the
bride and groom, which all could see but pretended not to
notice. It really was the first time in her life that Ajanti could
publicly indicate interest in someone of the opposite sex.

The next day was the time of farewell. Indian families trace
their descent in the male line, so when their women marry and

leave they are no longer really regarded as part of their own families but are joined to that of their husbands. Of course, in actual practice, parents feel the same way about their children as Westerners do, and visits home can and do occur. Nevertheless, the time that the bride leaves for her new home is a solemn one. Her father tells her to be good and never disgrace him by poor conduct. At the same time her family reiterates their love for her. Sad songs are sung and while they go on, the father gives his daughter away to her new family.

When we cleared Ajanti's village, she was riding on a brightly decorated donkey, and I could distinctly hear her sobbing beneath her veil. But it wasn't long before Gupta Das turned her sobs to happy talk.

Many Indian sons bring their brides to their parents' home and live with the parents even after they have children. This is because the eldest male is regarded as father of them all, and as such he rules the household. His sons inherit his property and upon his death the property, especially land, might be so divided up that it would be of advantage to no one. So through time Indian families have stayed together, sharing their total resources. This is often a difficult situation for a new bride, because she really doesn't have a home of her own. She has to obey her mother-in-law in all things. Certainly some noisy quarrels result later when children come into the home. But somehow these things usually work out, especially since there always seems to be someone to moderate an argument.

In fact, Indian villages govern their affairs very well by a kind of democratic system. There is a headman in each village who usually is the wealthiest. He acts as general administrator and moderator. He consults with a body of men, each of whom is usually the headman in his caste. Most of the village castes are represented in this body, which is called the *panchayat*. The headman and the panchayat run the village, and woe betide the individual who runs against their rulings. For such a man or woman can be held up to scorn by the entire village, which not only makes one uncomfortable, but also just might cut off his means of subsistence and force him to leave, becoming a kind of renegade. Disgrace is brought on his family at the same time, and they suffer as much as the culprit. This kind of administration is in many ways more effective than government laws, one reason why India's villages have lasted for so many thousands of years.

Heroes, Gods, and Yogis

High on a mountain-top before him, gleaming in inconceivable loveliness of level terraces and soaring spires, he saw the famous city of Lanka . . . It was, in truth, like some dwelling-place of the gods. Its many-storied buildings and fretted screens were studded with crystal. Great archways and splendid gates lent it their grandeur in all directions. Its streets and roadways were broad and well-cared for. Magnificent were its towers of victory. Beautiful were its lantern pillars. Its houses were like palaces, and its tombs like dainty marble canopies. Wonderful, verily, was this Lanka, famous throughout the world, ruled over by the might of Ravana, and vigilantly guarded by night-rangers of terrible strength. Oppressed by the thought of this glory Hanumant became sunk in gloom; when suddenly, as if on purpose to comfort him, the full moon arose in all her splendour with the stars. And the great monkey looking up, saw her, lovely with the sheen of a white conch-shell, wearing the tint of a white lotus, arisen and afloat in the heavens, like a beautiful swan swimming in a lake . . . RAMAYANA

For centuries in the evenings Indian families have gathered around the storyteller, who might more often than not be one of the old grandparents, but sometimes a wandering professional. No matter how wearying the day's labors, in the evening the world would become a rich and magical place as seen through

47

the storyteller's eyes. Wondrous tales of battles between gods and demons, of lost love and found love, of mortal heroes in strange lands, of treasures beyond price heaped up in the halls of golden palaces, of the origin of the world and the triumph of good over evil, of human failings and the all-seeing gods, of snakes, tigers, bears, peacocks, elephants, and monkeys, and of the rewards given men for doing the right things. These tales, told vividly, painted in a thousand colors, have been passed down from generation to generation. Though they vary in the telling, most of the details and all of the plots have remained the same for an incredibly long time.

One reason why these stories have lasted so long is that they are not only good tales, but most of them are intimately bound up with the religion of most of the people, that is, Hinduism. Usually books about India describe the religion of the Hindus in its very formal terms, but the religion of the villages is often quite different in its practical observance. Since India is a land of villages, the village version of Hinduism is the most important of all.

For instance, Pochamma, the strange goddess who brings smallpox, is rarely mentioned in standard works on Hinduism, but she is widely worshiped in India. Each year there is a festival to her, during which goats and sheep are sacrificed and new rice offered before her shrine. Everyone contributes to these sacrifices, even the Moslems. There is a goddess of cholera and even one of chicken pox, and both of these are annually worshiped during festivals. And there are other village goddesses whose powers control the health and general luck of the people. It is the job of the people to keep the gods happy and content so they won't get angry, and to appease their anger if it should appear. Doctors often find that the cures they offer for diseases are turned down by people who believe that only through worship can their ailments be overcome.

The village world is also full of ghosts and spirits. People who die suddenly because of accidents or suicide are said to haunt certain areas usually on the scene of the disaster. In one village, for example, there is the ghost of an old woman who died of snake bite near a large banyan tree. She appears to villagers toward evening when they are returning from the fields. It is said that she cackles and moans and tries to pull people into the tree but has not succeeded so far. Nevertheless, the tree is given a wide berth even at noontime.

Witchcraft, sorcery, black magic, are also known and there are usually several people among the villagers who are accredited with strange powers. There are even lively spirits in one's own family. These are ancestors who, being dissatisfied with their descendants' actions, plague them with all kinds of bad luck. There are also omens and signs which indicate good or bad luck when one starts a journey or tries a new crop.

The Brahmans, Mullah priests (Moslem), and others who have deep knowledge of such things advise people in these affairs. Ritual bathing, wearing of amulets, fasting, penitence, sacrifices, prayers, confessions, alms to the poor, even spell-casting and magic are some of the remedies employed against supernatural forces.

One of the very foolish things people from the West do is to laugh at such beliefs and call these village people ignorant. The ignorance is often on the Westerner's part, and it is worth a tale to say why.

Lal had a new plow. When the rain started he was among the first to hitch his oxen and start work in his fields. The furrows were being cut deep, and the new plow handled easily. My field will be ready quickly and my planting finished earlier than ever before, he thought as he drove his oxen on.

Suddenly there was a loud crack, and the long plow handle snapped in two.

Lal was very upset. He had no other recourse than to use his old worn-out plow. The new one could not be repaired in time to get his crops in.

Again, he set to work plowing. His work was slower this time, and the earth seemed harder. Even the rains had stopped, and the burning white sun beat down. Suddenly, another loud crack, and again the plow handle snapped off. His old plow had broken beyond repair.

What was he to do? Only a few hours before, he had counted himself one of the most fortunate men on earth, and now he was among the most miserable.

Sadly Lal returned to the village. His little son and daughter ran to him in hopes of play, but he walked by without looking at them. The women at the well stopped their chatter and watched him. Why was Lal going to the village when all men were in the fields at this time of day?

Lal knew there was only one thing to do. He was being punished by some force. And it was not just an ordinary witch or ghost but something stronger, perhaps Durga, the goddess of the earth. Lal shuddered, for Durga could destroy him and his family with the wink of her fierce eye. Already disaster had struck, for if he couldn't get his field plowed in time, his plants would never flourish and his family would starve. He had to see the Brahman, who could tell him what to do.

Mammata, the Brahman priest, was a member of the village panchayat and one of the most respected men in the village. Nevertheless, when quarrels broke out and families became disorderly, even Mammata was hard put to set things aright.

Lal came to him. First humbly kissing the hem of Mammata's robe, Lal squatted on the ground before the old priest. "In the name of all the gods, Lord Mammata, why am I plagued so?" he began his story.

Mammata listened gravely as Lal recounted the disastrous

events of the day. When he had finished, Mammata said: "Go home and try to repair your plow. Return tomorrow with the sun, and I will tell you what to do."

Lal did as he was told. Already relieved somewhat because he had explained his troubles to another, he was comforted to know that the pious Mammata, who knew the strange secrets of the world, could help him. Still he was cursed with ill fortune and there were tears in his house that night.

By Western standards Mammata was an ignorant man. He knew nothing of the world. He was awed by automobiles and airplanes, and things like vaccinations and sanitation seemed wrong because they went against tradition. But Mammata did know his village, which was all he needed to know. For thousands of years the people had turned to their seers and their priests in times of trouble with the knowledge that through them something would be done. A true Indian does not stoically accept his fate; he tries to do something about it.

Mammata offered a prayer to Siva, the viewer of all things. Then he went over the facts of Lal's case. There was no doubt that Lal had offended some powerful force. But what was the nature of his offense? Mammata knew the village—its gossip, its tensions, its friendships, its enemies, its daily problems. Lately from Lal's house there had frequently come the sound of quarreling. Though a hard-working man, Lal was also hot-tempered. He had been known to throw things, not only at his wife but even at neighbors. More than once his caste leaders had warned him about this. His family affairs were his own, but if they got outside his family, then he was disgracing not only himself and his family but his caste and the whole village as well. Such disgrace would offend many deities, including the village gods, but especially his family god and his ancestor-spirits. Clearly Lal owed his family an apology and a penance.

When Mammata told Lal his diagnosis, Lal felt deep shame.

Mammata went on to describe how everyone knew Lal's family affairs because his angry voice was the loudest in the village. No wonder his ancestors were angry and caused him mischief, no wonder his family god was ready to destroy his source of food. He had disgraced them all. Had not Lal's father, the strong Dandin, instructed him in the right way? Was not Lal aware that his present deeds would determine his next life?

Lal had to apologize to his ancestors before his whole family. He sacrificed a chicken to the family god, and called upon gods and ancestors to witness his self-control in future.

Meanwhile, Mammata had talked with other members of the panchayat and advised giving help to Lal. "For a starving family in our midst is as much a disgrace in our village as one that has too much." Another plow was lent to Lal while his new one was repaired. From then on the Lal house was known for its following of the right way.

This story is a good one because it shows the efficient way religion and economic need can work together. One might think that Mammata was an exceptional person, but quite the contrary; no Brahman, seer, or other leader could hold his place in village society for long without producing satisfactory answers to problems placed before him.

You will notice that Mammata put a great deal of emphasis upon "doing the right thing." This idea is summed up in the word *dharma,* or "that which is right." So fundamental is this idea to Indian religion that once one has it clearly in mind, it becomes possible to understand much of Indian life. "That which is right" includes things in daily life, like respecting elders and doing one's caste occupation. It also includes worshiping the gods by observing the festivals, fasting, sacrificing, and upholding caste customs. Holy pilgrimages to sacred rivers like the Ganges are dharma, as are obedience to laws, and doing the proper rituals at births, deaths, and marriages. Men such as Mammata really direct the villagers in the following of dharma.

"We shall have to account for our actions before God. We can deceive our family, our village, our caste, but we can never deceive God." This is probably the most repeated and well-known saying in India. It is acknowledged by Hindu, Moslem, Sikh, Jain, and Parsee alike. For the Hindu it has a special meaning. All Hindus believe that men have souls and that these are their real selves. These souls have existed before this life and will exist after it. The soul never dies, but it does undergo trials and triumphs, for it is part of an almost endless cycle. Frequently this cycle is depicted as a great wheel, continually turning, inside of which souls go from life to life.

"To be born is certain death, to the dead, birth is certain."

But if you look closely inside the wheel, you will notice that there are animals, birds, fish, insects, and reptiles as well as humans shown. You can see, too, that some of the humans are rich, some poor, some happy, and others miserable. To the Hindu, this wheel depicts his own soul's life cycle. In his next life he could be any of the animals or humans inside the wheel, depending on how good or bad he has been in this life. Failure to observe dharma might mean that in the next life his soul would be forced to live as a rat or perhaps as a leper. But good deeds or close attention to dharma must make the next life a better one than the present. Of course, what you are now was brought about by what you did in your previous existence. The Hindus call this sequence of lives *karma,* a very famous and important idea in the East. The movement of souls from form to form is called *transmigration,* also a very important term.

Hindus consider karma as something to escape from if one can. There is one escape which is no escape, and that is when one does real evil and is punished by being sent to hell. Hell is an awful place of fire, maggots, and reptiles from which none can get away. On the other hand, there is heaven, where one lives forever in a fine palace with marvelous servants and the best of everything. Of course, heaven isn't easy to attain; only the purest good go there and such goodness can only be obtained by constantly working for God. The following appears in the *Bhagavad-Gita:* "Cast all your acts upon me, with your mind on the Highest Soul. Have done with craving and selfhood."

The old sayings instruct people by holding up the highest ideals before them, and here the storyteller does a real service, especially to children. For so many of his stories have to do with the triumph of good over evil that practically from babyhood a child is given a very clear idea of what "doing the right thing" really is. As Mammata told Lal, "There is no excuse for doing something that is wrong. You have always known what is good and what is bad, so act accordingly, for God sees all."

God in India is not really the One God of Christianity or Judaism, or the Allah of the Moslems, though in the very highest Hindu teachings He might be said to be so. Hindus usually mean either Vishnu or Siva when they speak of God, for even in a religion of many gods these two have the greatest importance. One of the very interesting things about Hinduism is its tolerance for other religions. The Hindus very rarely have attempted to destroy another faith, but have expanded their own religion to include the other belief. So along with Vishnu and Siva, there are many other gods acknowledged, many of whom are no longer worshiped, but since they were popular in the past are still part of the pantheon. Even Buddha and Christ have places in Hinduism! "The gods are but different views of the same God," say Hindu sages.

The first time I encountered Siva was in the home of a

Hindu gentleman near the city of Madras in southeastern India. In one room of his house there stood an ancient bronze statue of a dancing figure. "Lord of the Dance," my friend called it. The figure stood on one foot; the other was raised in the air. Its four arms were poised as if to hold the body in perfect balance, and all around was a bronze frame representing a halo of flames. It did not take long to see what a wonderful statue it was. For the artist had understood fine dancing and had so gracefully created his statue that it seemed to whirl while standing still, something like a perfectly balanced top which is whirling so fast that it doesn't appear to be moving at all. This was one form of Siva, a young dancing man who is Lord of Stillness and of Motion at the same time. Since everything in the world has both these qualities—whether we are thinking of the solar system or the structure of the earth or of life itself—Siva is also Lord of the World.

The people of the villages realize this about Siva because their own lives are so closely connected with the soil. Any farmer knows that life and death are very closely bound together; without one, you cannot have another. People eat animals and plants which have to die so that people may live. In nature, dead beasts enrich the soil with their bodies and thus bring life to the plants on which animals feed. So Siva's dance represents death in its stillness and life in its motion, both at the same time.

Siva really is a farmer's god, and his symbols and those of his wife Parvati occur all over India. People worship them and have festivals in their honor.

Most of the images of Siva and Parvati have to do with the fertility of the earth and of man. Everything is bound up in the ideas of life and death, creation and destruction. Keep these things in mind when you look at the art of India, and you will understand why artists have added so many arms

and faces to their statues; they are really trying to show how great and numerous are the powers of the gods. Whatever aspect of the god you wish to see, it is there; you only need to look and think while looking, and it will appear.

For example, Parvati is a beautiful woman whose sheer goodness was such that Siva, who usually is above such things, fell in love with her and they married. But just as Siva has many forms, some terrifying and destructive and others gentle and creative, so with his wife. Sometimes she is the lovely Sati, the virtuous lady, but on other occasions she is Durga, the war goddess, a horrible old woman with dozens of weapon-carrying arms, and a hideous face full of tusks, bulging eyes, and a bloody mouth!

Siva and Parvati had two famous sons, one Skanda, the god of war, and the other the delightful elephant-headed god, Ganesha, who is one of the most popular deities in India. Ganesha brings good fortune and helps overcome problems and obstacles. It is no wonder that many Indian officials keep a little figure of Ganesha on their desks; perhaps he helps them surmount red tape!

Along the roads and in the holy cities like Benares, one sees almost naked men with wild hair, their bodies covered with gray ashes. These are the ascetics, some of whom we call *yogis*. Ascetics are men who try to eliminate the usual physical and mental instincts which we all have, in order to concentrate on truth. Now truth as they seek it is something beyond the understanding of men. Truth can only come from the Divine, and it is only by meditating on the Divine that truth can be learned. But true meditation requires self-discipline and complete body control, and this the ascetics try to achieve by various means, many of which require placing the body in positions which are painful at first but become less so with practice. In case this doesn't make too much sense to you, try thinking about something like circles inside circles, each one smaller than the other. How many circles can you count? Just remember, too, that when you get down to the smallest circle, there are still smaller circles beyond your perception and so on and on. You'll also notice if you try this, that it takes all your concentration to count the circles, and that the harder you try, the more difficult it becomes.

Now the yogi thinks of things like the circles as something whose riddle he can solve if he prepares his body and his mind so that there is no effort or frustration; then true ideas can flow from God to him. By physical training he controls his body. The famous yogi acrobatics, positions, and the like are part of this training. He also has to train himself in concentration, which he calls "steadying the mind." To do this he concentrates on solitary objects like a lotus or an image or even his toe. Eventually the yogis and other ascetics who use meditation come to feel they have found true knowledge, and this frees them from karma.

Some ascetics were great teachers and tried to help others. Some taught that the world around us is really an illusion. If you didn't know that the little figures on your TV screen were actors in a studio far away, then you might think of them as actually being in the set. The actors give the illusion of reality, but neither are they near you, nor is the action they are performing real. It is merely a play, a false reality. In the same way the ascetic teachers try to get people to look away from the world of illusion (the world around them) to the world of God, our world being but the faint shadow of the real world of God.

Siva is the patron saint of the ascetics and is frequently depicted in sculpture and painting as sitting on a tiger skin high up on Mount Kailasa in the Himalayas. He is in meditation and is shown covered with ashes and his long hair is matted. He has a topknot, however, which holds the crescent moon and which also is the source of the holy river Ganges. The eye in the middle of his forehead is the symbol of his all-seeing powers. Another symbol, the trident, is his favorite weapon, and a great bull is usually near-by. This is Nandi, upon whom Siva rides. Nandi is also worshiped in India, and one finds bull images everywhere.

In spite of Siva's vast powers and useful functions, he seems more than a little dangerous. There is a story told of the time that the gods were very much upset because a demon was threatening to destroy heaven. Brahma, the father of the gods, told them that the demon could only be defeated by a son of Siva. But Siva was not married and he had no son. Parvati was then a beautiful young princess who had always loved Siva and so was ideally suited to be Siva's bride. But Siva knew nothing of her, since he was always meditating, and of course he knew nothing of love. Besides, he was so formidable that no one, not even the gods, liked to approach him. But the gods were desperate, and they instructed Kama, the archer god of love, to shoot one of his arrows into Siva's heart so that when he saw Parvati he would fall in love immediately. Kama discussed the matter with his wife Roti, or Desire, and they both trembled at the audacity of the idea. For Siva would certainly be angry. Kama's arrows were meant for humans, not gods, and especially not for Siva, the great yogi.

But what had to be done had to be done. With the aid of the god of spring they found Siva meditating in a forest. Parvati had come there to pray to him, so conditions were ideal. Siva, who always smiles upon his true worshipers, smiled upon Parvati and as he did so, Kama bent his bow. But before he could release his arrow, Siva the all-knowing became aware of the situation and his third eye opened and burned poor Kama into ashes! Siva then vanished.

Kama's wife Roti was grief-stricken and as all good wives were supposed to do, she and the god of spring built a funeral fire and she prepared to jump into the flames in order to follow her dead husband. This was a very common practice for wives in India before the British brought reform and was known as *suttee*. But the god of the sky, Indra, stopped her and told her that Siva would marry Parvati after all and then would restore Kama to her. Sure enough, it happened that way and Kama was restored to life. But since his body had been destroyed, he was now invisible to men, the reason why love can't be seen as he moves about shooting his arrows. His bow is a stalk of sugar cane, his bowstring a line of bees, and his arrows are flowers!

Vishnu is a wonderful god. Vishnu is all things. Indian villagers consider him the creator of the world, and he is also its guardian. He can do everything Siva can do, and yet he doesn't seem to be dangerous but rather loving and merciful.

> I am unending time
> I am destroying death
> I am victory, I am courage
> I am the goodness of the virtuous
> I am the silence of what is secret
> I am the seed of all that is born
>   There is no end to my
> holy powers. . . . and whatever is mighty or fortunate or
> strong, springs from a portion of my glory
>
> —*Bhagavad-Gita*

Vishnu slept on a thousand-headed snake in a great ocean. While he slept a lotus grew out of his navel, and in this lotus was born the creator god Brahma. Brahma created the world, and then Vishnu went to heaven to rule the whole universe. Vishnu and his wife, the beautiful Lakshmi, never lost their concern about the world and every time some terrible thing was about to happen to it, Vishnu would appear in some form to save it. These forms are called *avatars,* or incarnations, and there are ten principal ones.

Once the whole world was to be flooded, so Vishnu took the form of a fish and warned Manu, the first man created by the gods, according to tradition, and thus the Adam of India. When the flood came Vishnu carried Manu's ship on his back and saved him and all his family, just as in the Biblical story of Noah.

At the very beginning of this chapter there is an excerpt from the *Ramayana,* one of the two great epic poems of India —poems whose stories are favorites above all stories. The *Ramayana* tells of the time the demon Ravana oppressed the world from his kingdom in Ceylon (Lanka). Vishnu incarnated himself as Rama, the handsome young prince of Ayodhya. Ravana stole away Sita, Rama's wife, and imprisoned her in his palace in Ceylon. Rama and his brothers set out to rescue her, aided in this by the bears and the monkeys. One of these monkeys was Hanumant, who became a very close friend of Rama and was the one to find Sita and give her courage. In his honor, monkeys are held as sacred in many parts of India and regarded as loyal guardians of the villages. Eventually, after a terrible battle, Rama and his allies destroyed Ravana and his demons, and Sita was restored to her husband. Throughout all these trials Rama and Sita stand out as ideals for husband and wife. Rama is a brave and just prince, and

his brothers are loyal and faithful. The *Ramayana* has many
of the high qualities of King Arthur and his Knights, and it is
a wonderful story by any standard.

Krishna is the favorite incarnation of Vishnu. He was born
to his father and mother while both were in prison. They had
been placed there because the ruling king of the country had
heard a prophecy that a child of these two people would kill
him, so he destroyed each one as soon as it was born. Krishna,
however, was smuggled out and brought up as the son of a
cowherd. As a baby he was a rather uncomfortable child to
have around, for even as an infant he would sometimes pull
down giant trees or catch the spirit out of the whirlwind. But
his foster mother loved and took good care of him, even
spanking him when he was naughty. Since as Vishnu he really
was also Lord of the Universe, the idea that he would submit
to a spanking and cry is one of the delightful parts of the
story. Baba (Baby) Krishna has a warm place in the hearts of
Indian women even today, particularly among mothers, and it
is easy to understand why. You can buy a little statue of Baba
Krishna almost anywhere in India. It is very easy to recognize,
for it is simply a fat baby crawling on all fours, just about to
get into mischief.

When Krishna was a little older he went out every day with
his friends, the boy and girl cowherds. Out in the forest and
pastures he played like any boy: swimming, chasing, and
playing pranks. Of course he performed occasional miracles
like raising a mountain with one hand or destroying fantastic
demons, but he always seemed to subside into an almost
normal boy again and play about with as much nonsense as
ever. He was a remarkable flute player and all the girl cowherds danced to his music and fell in love with him. One girl,
the beautiful Radha, fell very deeply in love with him, but
aware that he was a god, she knew they could never marry.

However, Krishna also loved her and as a result there is a tradition in India that love is a special way in which humans can communicate with divinity. Partly to symbolize this, Indian cultists make a wonderful image of Krishna as a handsome young man standing with his legs crossed under a tree and playing his flute. The notes of the flute call all men to love God.

When the wonderful days of youth among the cowherds were at an end Krishna came into his own as a royal prince. He destroyed the wicked king and built a new kingdom celebrated for its justice and its beauty. Krishna married and is said to have had 16,000 wives besides his chief queen Rukmini; and he was father of over 180,000 sons! He had to fight and destroy evil demons all over India, and he gradually made it a happier land as he won victory after victory. But even though he was a god, the later years of his rule were not very pleasant ones.

Those years are described in the second great epic poem of India, called the *Mahabharata*. It is a veritable mine of fine stories, chief among which is the account of the struggle for control of India between the Kauravas and their cousins, the five Pandavas. The Pandavas were fine princes and one of them, Arjuna, was a close friend of Krishna. But the Kauravas continued to persecute the Pandava brothers until finally civil war broke out. A terrible battle was fought near Delhi. It is said that every ruler in India, and even the Greeks and the Chinese, took part in the struggle. Krishna was charioteer for Arjuna, and he encouraged the Pandavas throughout the eighteen days it took to reach a decision. At last the battle was over, but not until all the leaders and most of the armies were annihilated. Only the five brothers and Krishna were left. The women of the defeated Kauravas were left to weep over their fallen husbands, brothers, and sons. The queen mother lamented and questioned as all mothers have cried out in time of war: "Why does not my heart break into a hundred pieces at the sight of my beloved killed in battle? What sins have I and these other daughters of men committed, that time should bring this disaster upon us?"

Krishna comforted the women by pointing out that each person is born into the world to carry out his job. The laborer to work, and royal princes to fight and die. Here is one of the tenets of the caste system repeated in this famous story.

Krishna himself realized that his own kingdom was destined to collapse even though his friends, the Pandavas, were now in power and were to be fine rulers. Indeed, Krishna's kingdom was destroyed by civil war and Krishna's best-loved son and his own brother were killed along with his friends. At last the great king wandered alone in the forest, grieving over all that had happened. He lay down to rest and a hunter, mistaking him for a deer, shot an arrow into his heel—his one vulnerable spot. Krishna died, forgiving his slayer, and his ruined kingdom was covered by the sea.

It is a fine story and one which every child in India knows, whether he be Hindu, Moslem, or Christian. Krishna has probably inspired more artists than any other, and some of the finest poetry ever written in the East can be traced to his story.

Vishnu is said also to have incarnated himself as Buddha in order to bring mercy to animals. Apparently he is not finished with the world either, for many Hindus believe that he will again appear as Kalkin, a man on a white horse ready to reward goodness and punish evil.

The last time I was in an Indian village it was September and the crops were growing rapidly toward full ripening. It was a good time, for the villagers felt assured of their food supply for another year. Very early one morning I heard the steady jingle of a woman's anklets, and on the wall of my room I saw flickers of reflected light. I rose and looked into the next room. There the lady of the house was dancing before her husband. She held a flickering lamp and bowed and swayed before him as if he were the image of a god. Later I learned that that is exactly what this rite really signified. The man was like Vishnu, creator and preserver of his family; the woman, his wife, was like Lakshmi acknowledging her husband's powers.

That evening and the next, lamps were set in rows before each house. Cattle moved about in the shadows, their skins painted with all kinds of designs, gentle bells tinkling from their necks. People everywhere laughed quietly, feasted on the nicest things they could obtain, and kept bringing some of these delicacies before the images of Lakshmi to offer her a share of their good fortune of that year. For this Festival of Lights was really for her. She represented not only their good luck and prosperity, but at the same time she was the gentle, faithful lady-wife of Vishnu, who by love and strength won good for all men. This quality of India's ancient religion is something that links East and West very closely indeed.

Most Ancient India

Deep in the jungles and buried in the distant places of India, there still survive primitive people whose way of life closely resembles that of their ancestors of thousands of years ago. Once they were the sole rulers of India, but now they survive only in isolated places. Our account has very little to do with these people, but we have to acknowledge their contribution to India's story, for they have left their traces there.

In very ancient times only hunters roamed over India. It must have been a hunter's paradise then, even though a dangerous one. The forests and plains were filled with deer and buffalo, game birds flocked in plenty, and the streams and lakes were rich with fish. Fruits, nuts, and herbs were certainly available, and there were flowers and fine-smelling woods for those who liked such things.

But at the same time, India was the home of the tiger and the leopard; of the rhinoceros and the elephant; of fierce buffalo and man-eating crocodiles; of snakes like the colorful, deadly krait, the saw-scaled viper, and above all the most royal of poisonous snakes, the cobra. These beasts command anyone's respect, and there is no doubt that the primitive hunters of India held them in great awe, even to the extent of worshiping some of them as spirit powers. That is probably why even today many Hindus still regard cobras, elephants and even certain trees, mountains, and rivers as sacred, and worship them. This worship harks back to the very beginnings of religion in India.

These primitive people may have contributed other things to India's culture. Perhaps they were the first to build homes on stilts, to make cloth out of bark, to tattoo, and to form musical instruments out of gourds. We don't know for sure, of course, but one thing is certain: such things have been used in India for a long, long time.

Hard work by archaeologists is beginning to prove that farming first came into the world in the Near East somewhere around 9000 to 7000 B.C. In the lands sometimes known as the Fertile Crescent, wheat-growing and animal domestication allowed people who had formerly lived as hunters to settle into villages and live their whole lives in the same place, free from the fear of starvation. Now, living together means that people who have ideas about doing or making things can exchange their ideas with others and so improve their own methods. In this way the farmers of the ancient Near East seem to have invented and developed such things as the animal-drawn plow, the hoe, and the techniques of weaving, making bricks, and constructing mud houses. Later they learned how to irrigate their fields with water, to use copper, to make pottery; and they discovered the use of the wheel and the lever. By 3500 B.C. in Egypt and Sumeria the farmers had developed so far that they were ready to take the final step to civilization.

Civilization really means having such a plentiful source of food that society can support a large number of people who do not have to farm but can do other work instead, like pottery making, metalworking and stonecutting, or being priests, soldiers, officials, and rulers. These non-farmers usually live in cities and towns, and because their activities are so numerous and complicated, societies eventually begin to develop writing and counting systems, law codes, classes, and even build enormous temples, tombs, and palaces. These developments are important parts of civilization; and in Sumeria, for example, cities like Babylon and Ur became the centers of all activity. Even the farmers came into the cities every night after the day's labor. Around 3000 B.C. civilization, fully developed, was beginning to change the world!

It is necessary to know what had occurred in the Near East in order to understand what happened to create ancient Indian civilization. In those thousands of years after agriculture was born, populations increased where farming was productive. This was one reason why farmers were always expanding their fields and trying to control water and fertility. The early farmers had to learn the hard way and were not always successful, by any means. One thing they learned was that they could not grow crops in the same place every year without doing something about fertilizing the soil. This some did, but others moved away and found new fields. Thus for various reasons farming spread out of the Near East, moving into Europe and across Asia.

If you travel up into the desert Plateau of Iran and go eastward, in almost every valley where there is water and cultivable soil you will find not only a modern village, but a mound or two to mark the heaped-up remains of ancient villages. These ancient villages are the signposts of a migration of people and ideas as great as the westward movement in the United States of coon-skin hunters and covered wagons. It took these early people much longer than the American pioneers; but eventually—after thousands of years—their descendants, not really knowing where they were or what they had reached, came down into the great valley of the Indus River and into a different world from the arid plateau it had taken so many generations to cross.

On the borders of the Indus Valley, I had the opportunity

to do some archaeological exploring, and in one valley which leads to the Indus from various parts of inner Asia we came upon a great many ancient mounds. We dug into some of these and discovered that the first farming people there arrived around 4000 B.C. and that although they didn't have pottery, they had plenty of sheep and goats. They lived in crude adobe huts and probably had very small fields.

As people in Iran learned new techniques they passed them on, either by coming to the region and settling or simply by passing along ideas through talk and demonstration. So in our valley we found that the villages became more numerous and the houses were much better made. Stone in the foundations, brick in the walls, even stone sockets to swing doors on. And here had been made some of the finest pottery in the world. All varieties of shapes painted in wonderful geometric designs or with stylized plants and animals lined up in horizontal rows. Some of these animals—like the ibex—were native to Iran, but others—the humped bull, for instance—belong to India. Here, then, is where India and the Near East met.

At last, at the very top of one large mound we found a great platform in the corner of which was a human skull. Someone had been sacrificed to provide an offering to the gods in order to dedicate the building properly. We found out something about those gods, for associated with the platform were clay figurines of bulls and of strange female goddesses. It seems obvious that these objects represent the worship of the powers of fertility just as those of Siva and his consort Parvati in Hinduism today. These discoveries of ours were probably of an ancient cult, an ancestor to Hinduism. But our valley and others like it were not rich enough to support the growth of civilization.

However, down in the Indus River valley two cities have

1"

been found dating around 2000 B.C. These cities, called Harappa and Mohenjo-daro, indicate that civilization did arrive at last in India perhaps a thousand years after its first development in the Fertile Crescent lands. This early Indian civilization was something quite different from that of the Tigris-Euphrates area. Remember that ideas traveled slowly across the fifteen hundred miles of desert that separates the Indus from those great rivers. Remember too that in the valley where we had dug we found traces of a long development where the ideas of East and West seem to have blended.

Old villages are found everywhere in the Indus valley, and these seem to have been the support for the cities. The villagers here did not live in the cities as they did in Sumeria but were content with their village life. On occasion they came to the cities to worship, for Mohenjo-daro and Harappa appear to

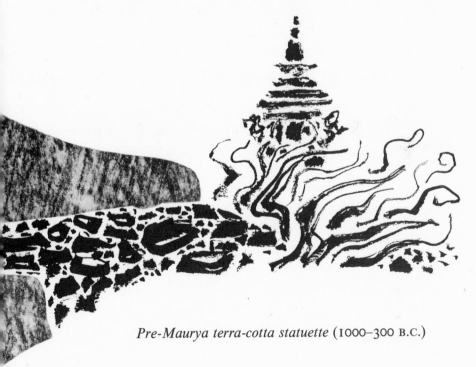

Pre-Maurya terra-cotta statuette (1000–300 B.C.)

have been temple cities with many priests, and of course warehouses to store the food the villagers brought.

What places they must have been! Enormous buildings of fired brick laid out in rows; temples and warehouses on heights, priests' and other people's quarters around them. Along some of the alleys and streets, covered sewers handled the run-off from drains in the houses or from a great ritual bathhouse. The priests wore cotton cloth—Indians were the first to use cotton—and probably wore rectangular seals on strings around their necks. There is writing on these seals, but so far no one has managed to translate it.

Archaeologists have found a great many clay figurines of bulls and mother goddesses even more elaborate than the ones we found in our valley. Little clay carts and some funny animal whistles were probably toys which every culture has, no matter where or when it lived. Clay images of cows indicate that the cow may have been held sacred, most likely because of her fine milk which nourished man. If that is true, we have the origin of the modern Hindu belief in the cow's holiness, one reason why this animal walks unmolested through the streets of villages and cities all over India.

There is a great deal in this old Harappan civilization to remind us of modern Indian life. A fine dancing girl with bangles on her arms, the figurines and carvings of great humped bulls, and the wide horns of the water buffalo, clay legs for cooking pots, even a god with three faces! Here along the Indus River Indian civilization really got its start.

The farmers were not content with the Indus valley alone. There was much to disturb them there, including floods and water-logging of the soil. The Harappan civilization spread with the farmers south to the banks of the Narbada, beyond the swamps of the Rann of Cutch, and north and east around the terrible desert of Thar deep into the rich country of the

Land of Five Rivers: the Punjab. At last to the Ganges, even beyond the place where the fabulous city of Delhi was to grow. But there came an end to this expansion. The farther one went south and east, the more difficult it was to grow the grain upon which the people depended; the climate is too hot and moist.

This problem was overcome, however, with the development of rice cultivation sometime after 1500 B.C. Rice may have first been cultivated in South China or in Thailand or Burma, but once it was accomplished, the whole vast region of tropical Asia was opened to the farmer. This probably was one major reason why the old Indian civilization on the banks of the Indus River died, but there were other reasons as well for its death.

In central Asia nomadic peoples were pressing in on one another in their search for new fields and pastures. Some of these spilled over into the lands ruled by the old Indus River civilizations. Wars broke out, but the newcomers were fierce warriors who possessed the horse and chariot and in a very short time they were owners of large empires.

A group of these people called the Aryans, speaking a language related to Greek and Persian, came through the mountains of Afghanistan and by means of such famous passes as the Khyber, located in the northwest, moved into India. Whether or not they found the Harappan civilization already floundering is still uncertain, but in any case they and allied peoples of the hills appear to have destroyed what was left. It must have been many centuries before these invasions ceased. It was a time of tribes, not of cities, and we know very little about life then. We would know even less except for an extraordinary thing.

The great respect which religion holds in India insures the long survival of such things as hymns and rituals. Incredible as it may seem, hymns composed at the time the Aryans ruled North India have survived virtually unchanged for three thousand years! More incredible is the fact that these hymns were not written down but were recited from memory and so passed, word for word, from generation to generation. Today these hymns are still used in Hindu rituals. They are called the Vedic hymns, and the earliest and most important of these is the *Rig Veda.* Later there were other works composed, such as the *Brahmanas* and the *Upanishads,* but it is the *Rig Veda* that tells us most about the times.

Those must have been violent and exciting days. The hymns tell us of constant wars, of cattle-raiding, and feats of daring. The horse was practically worshiped, as well he might be for his great contribution to Aryan success. Aryan families were built around the father, and the father owed allegiance to the tribe and the tribal chief. Classes developed as the Aryans conquered the old inhabitants of India. There were four of these in descending order: priests (Brahmans), warriors (Kshatriya), peasants (Vaisya), and serfs (Sudras). These classes made sure that each function necessary to their tribal survival and success was carried out. Organization must certainly have been necessary, for it appears that the Aryans not only loved to fight and race in their chariots, but drinking, music, and dice-playing were favorite pastimes. Aryan men had consciences, too, and sometimes regretted the trouble they got into. One fellow who couldn't stop gambling laments:

> Don't play with dice, but plough your furrow!
> Delight in your property, prize it highly!
> Look to your cattle and look to your wife,
> You gambler! . . .
> So make friends with us, be kind to us!
> Do not force us with your fierce magic!
> May your wrath and hatred now come to rest!
> May no man fall into the snares of the dice!

The Aryans worshiped gods of nature such as Indra, the god of the storm and of war who gave his name to India; Surya, the sun god who, like Apollo of the Greeks, dashes across the sky in a flaming sun chariot; and Ushas, the lovely goddess of the dawn. There were many gods, but only two others can we mention here: Agni, the god of fire who was everywhere—in the lightning, in the sacrificial flame, and in the family hearth; Varuna, who was king of the gods. Like Zeus, he was in charge of keeping order among gods and men. Varuna was all-seeing, and no sin could escape him.

Men kept the gods happy in those days by offering sacrifices during which *soma* (an alcoholic drink) was drunk and prayers and hymns recited. The Brahmans headed these affairs.

Gradually it appears that the Aryans settled down, though we know that great wars were still fought. These were wars between established kingdoms, rather than roving tribes. The war between the Kauravas and the Pandavas described in the *Mahabharata* may very well have been one of these conflicts. In any case, we know very little as yet about this period of the Aryans. But one thing is certain, and that is that the Aryan culture blended with the old cultures of India and made ready the scene for one of India's greatest men.

The Buddha and History

Every once in a while history suddenly glows, lighted by the life of someone who seems to stand outside the usual events of wars and revolutions which all too frequently make up the story of man. Believing so completely in wonderful ideas like justice, human dignity, the immortality of the soul, and the essential goodness of man, such men willingly give their lives as proof of their beliefs. Socrates and Jesus are great, great men of history. For India, it was Siddhartha Gautama, known as the Buddha.

Gautama was born about 560 B.C., the son of Suddhodhana, king of the Sakyas, a people of the Himalayan foothills. His mother was Mahamaya, and according to the traditional story, before Gautama was born she had a dream in which she was carried away to a sacred lake. By its shores she encountered a white elephant—carrying a lotus flower, symbol of purity, in its trunk—who entered her side.

Mahamaya told her dream to wise men. All but one stated that the dream meant that she would have a son who would be emperor of the world. But the one sage prophesied that her son would see four signs evidencing the misery of life, and these signs would make him not a ruler, but a teacher of the world.

The king did not want this last prophecy to come true. He saw to it that the little prince was raised in an atmosphere of absolute delight. His homes were wonderful palaces with great parks around them. Trained as a prince should be in all the arts of physical and mental skill, Gautama excelled in everything. He even won his beautiful cousin Yasodhara by overcoming all opponents in a wrestling contest. When he married her it was a time of great joy indeed.

But it appears that beneath his healthy, happy exterior the prince was not altogether content. Perhaps things came too easy for him. Maybe the challenge of living had been taken from him by his having been given everything he wished. Here he was, a full-grown young man ready to meet the world, and there was nothing to meet! Why all this training? What good did it do if there was really nothing to use it for? The young prince became restless. He needed a goal in life, but he did not know what it would be.

Then one day in the royal park as he was driving about in his chariot, he came upon a very old man so burdened with his years that he could hardly move. The contrast between the vigorous young prince and this old man was very clear. Time eventually turns all youth into old age. All men must grow old and feeble. It is the destiny of those who are born. Gautama shuddered at the thought. "Why must this be?" his youth cried out against that fate.

Very soon afterward Gautama came upon a sick man shivering with fever, his skin covered with boils. The terrible misery of the sick struck hard upon the mind of the prince who had been aware only of happy, joyful, healthy things.

Again, a little later, another of the four signs revealed itself. Gautama heard crying, and there before his eyes passed a funeral procession, the dead man being carried on his funeral bier to the cremation ground, followed by his weeping family.

Old age, disease, death—what happiness could man really

have, with such things always destined for him? Was there no way out of man's terrible situation? Surely there must be! Yet every man at whom Gautama looked had marks of suffering on him, no matter how happy he might seem. To say that the young prince was troubled is to understate his feelings.

Then one day he saw a wandering ascetic, a man who had nothing more than a begging bowl to carry and a yellow robe to cover his body, but who gave no indication of suffering. Rather, he went peacefully about, completely happy in the harsh world. Here was the fourth sign prophesied.

Gautama knew that he too must go into the world and become a wandering ascetic. His father tried to dissuade him. He even put guards on his son, at the same time giving him greater luxuries than ever before. Yasodhara, Gautama's wife, gave birth to a son, an event that fills all fathers with joy; but Gautama found no pleasure in the news. Instead, that night while everyone else was celebrating, Gautama stole out of the palace. Saddling his favorite horse, Kanthaka, he rode away accompanied only by his charioteer, Channa.

Outside his father's city Gautama stopped. He dismounted from his horse and took off all his fine clothes and jewelry. He cut off his long hair with his sword and gave it to Channa to return with the other things to his father, the king. He patted his horse and bade him good-by. But according to the story, Kanthaka, overcome with grief at losing his good master, dropped dead. It is said that he was reborn in heaven soon afterward.

Gautama now lived the life of a wandering hermit. He talked with sages and ascetics, gradually learning how to meditate and acquiring the ancient wisdom of the Brahmans. But he was not content with this. He began to practice harsh things like self-starvation. For six years he tried to overcome his body's natural inclinations so that, as some ascetics believed, he might break free from the karma cycle. In fact, five ascetics made him their leader because he was so intent on doing this. When Gautama was almost nothing but skin and bones he realized that he wasn't getting anywhere at all. He gave up the starvation idea and began to eat again. Yet still he wandered, searching, listening, learning, and thinking.

At last he came to the town of Gaya where he sat in the shade of a fig tree—sometimes called the *bodhi* tree, or tree of "wisdom"—and looked back over his life. He was about thirty-five years old now—and what had he accomplished so far? What truth had he learned? He had been prince, hermit, ascetic, and beggar, but he was no nearer to settling his discontent than ever before. Gautama must have been very tired and certainly despairing. The young daughter of a local farmer brought him a big bowl of rice. It may have been then that he resolved, once and for all, to find an answer. Maybe it was the fact that in gazing at the fresh young face of the girl he could see the suffering that would be hers in life, even though she was good and innocent. At any rate, he vowed to remain seated under the tree until he solved the riddle of man's misery.

Buddhist artists loved to picture the next forty-nine days, for much as Jesus was tempted in the wilderness, so was Gautama. Mara, the Buddhist Satan, tried in every way possible to break Gautama's resolution. He flung storms at him; he called upon beautiful women to tempt him; he told him frightening news about his family; he shook him with earthquakes. All to no avail, and Mara finally gave up in disgust.

On the forty-ninth day Gautama knew at last why the world was full of sorrow and what man could do about it. He was now fully enlightened and thus became the Buddha or "The Awakened One."

With this awakening, Buddha was ready to teach, but he spent another seven weeks under his sacred tree thinking about what he had learned. At last he rose to his feet and went to the deer park outside the sacred city of Benares on the Ganges. There he preached to the five ascetics who had followed him in the days when he had led them in starvation. Soon he gathered about him disciples of every kind, from kings to hermits.

He wandered about India with his monks, teaching and converting. At last he returned to his home and there converted his whole family. His wicked cousin Devadatta tried to kill him by letting loose a mad elephant along the path Buddha was taking. But the colossal beast stopped his mad rush when he saw Buddha calmly strolling toward him, as fearless as the greatest warriors and yet as gentle as a tiny lamb, and the elephant then knelt in homage.

For over forty years Buddha went about the land, preaching. At last, at the age of eighty, tired and as aged as the old man he had seen in the park so long before, Buddha lay down under a tree. He instructed his grieving disciples to remember the sorrow of life and to work steadfastly teaching the truths they had learned. He then died peacefully, his full life completed. A life that uncounted millions of Asians have been influenced by even up to our own time.

But what was the great enlightenment? So many forms of Buddhism have arisen since Gautama's day that it is sometimes very difficult to find out what was the first Buddhism. Buddha's preaching was oral, and since very few people could read and write, there was no one to take down what he said.

It was only centuries after his death that much of his teaching was at last written down, and by that time of course, his actual words were probably somewhat changed. In fact, Buddhists got into arguments as to just what he did say about certain things, and this helped to lead to the formation of different kinds of Buddhism.

But in spite of all the complications that men have made of Buddha's teaching, the fundamental idea which Buddha taught remains the same. It is embodied in what are called the Noble Truths. It is that man's misery is caused by his craving for such things as wealth, power, love, and joy; and in pursuit of these he causes sorrow and brings misery upon himself. Men try to be individuals, separate from the divine spirit they all share in common. By not acknowledging their common ancestry, they stay as men—being born, living, and dying. The way out of man's suffering is to be neither an extreme craver nor an extreme ascetic, but rather to follow calmly a middle way, keeping to a responsible ordered life. Men can do this by following the Noble Eightfold Path:

1. Right Views
2. Right Resolve
3. Right Speech
4. Right Conduct
5. Right Livelihood
6. Right Effort
7. Right Recollection
8. Right Meditation

Buddha apparently laid down rules by which his followers could live. He may also have discussed with them the whole plan of the universe. He seems to have told them that he was only one of a line of Buddhas, all of whom existed before him, bringing enlightenment to the world. Centuries after his death the idea developed that another Buddha would be born, and so the cult of the Coming Buddha came into being. This cult is especially important in Japan.

One idea the followers of Buddha developed was that of Nirvana, which is the place or state one reaches when one has successfully followed the Middle Way. It can be called a kind of heaven, though its essential quality is calmness and purity, rather than the unbounded joy that we in the West would like heaven to be. But certainly it is a wonderful place to attain.

One important school of Buddhism, called the Lesser Vehicle, taught that each man must find his own way to salvation. The way, of course, being to follow closely the teachings of Gautama Buddha. These teachings were written down into a kind of bible called the Three Baskets. It got such a name because there were three essential parts to the teachings, and all three had been written down on palm leaves—Indian paper —and then stored in three baskets, the most convenient bookcases.

One part of the third of the Three Baskets contains stories of the various incarnations Buddha underwent before his last and greatest one. These incarnations are called "Jatakas," and they are among the loveliest stories ever written. In them Buddha has the form of a heavenly being called a *bodhisattva,* who becomes an animal or a man according to the incarnation. In all of them the hero sacrifices himself for others. The king of the deer gives himself up to the hunters so that the rest of the herd can escape; the parrot tries to save his brothers from the forest fire by scattering drops of water from his little wings on the holocaust below, and failing, gives up his life in the attempt; King Sivi saves a pigeon from a hawk by giving

the equivalent of his own flesh. Here goodness is more lasting than any other quality, and Buddhists everywhere revere these stories.

One trouble with Three Basket Buddhism is that for common men it is very hard to steer a middle course, and so they keep on suffering. But surely, reasoned some wise men, the kindly, merciful bodhisattvas of the Jataka tales would not be content to rest in heaven while men and animals continue to suffer on earth. Besides, it seems awfully selfish for the men who have the ability to go to heaven simply to go, without thinking of the rest of mankind. Heaven would then be a place only for the selfish.

Out of this kind of reasoning developed a whole new school of Buddhism, one that spread farther than even Buddha himself might have conceived. This Buddhism is called the Great Vehicle, and whereas the Lesser Vehicle only exists today in Ceylon, Burma, and Thailand, the Great Vehicle spreads across Asia to Japan and for a period of time it was the state religion of mighty China. It is an appealing Buddhism, for it describes the universe as filled with compassionate bodhisattvas with different powers, but all of whom are concerned with saving all living things. Some refuse to go to heaven and instead, out of their goodness, assume man's sufferings. The bodhisattva resolves: ". . . I take upon myself all the sorrows of all beings. I resolve to bear every torment in every purgatory of the universe. For it is better that I alone suffer than the multitude of living beings. I give myself in exchange . . ."

This tenet has much in common with Christianity, and it is not unlikely that this form of Buddhism owes a great deal to the teachings of Jesus which had already reached India by the time the Great Vehicle was formed.

Of course, Buddhism is not as simple as it seems; there are

all kinds of ideas and philosophical thoughts involved in it, many of which Gautama himself would probably not understand, so far away from his teachings have men frequently come. But certain it is that he would approve of the teaching of the Noble Eightfold Path and of the Four Cardinal Virtues: pity, serenity, joy, and love. "Just as a mother, as long as she lives, cares for her only child, so should a man feel all-embracing love to all living beings."

The impact of Buddhism on India was a very great one, and it is strange that, today, in the land of Buddha's birth, Buddhism has almost completely disappeared. Yet while it existed, it carved immortal traces on the culture of its homeland.

Other religions began in India about the time of the Buddha. One of these, Jainism, was begun by a man named Mahavira (The Great Hero), and it still survives. One important part of Jainism is the protection of all life, even insects, and the Jains go to great lengths to avoid killing anything.

Buddha's life was centered in a group of little countries along the Ganges River. These countries were always quarreling and trying to conquer one another. About the time of the "enlightenment" at Gaya, the great Persian King Darius I conquered part of the Punjab, but India was little affected by Persian civilization.

Alexander the Great opened the way. Smashing the Persians, he marched into the Punjab and set out for the Ganges. But after winning a fearful battle with Porus, the powerful Indian king, Alexander's men refused to march farther. The world was too strange and their homes too far away. Alexander had to turn back, but first he marched down the Indus River to the sea, where he built a fleet to sail part of his army home. The accounts of Alexander's campaigns written by Greeks and later by Romans opened Western men's eyes to the riches of India, and as time went on men dreamed of India as a land of limitless wealth, a dream that was to have serious consequences for that troubled land.

Soon after Alexander's death and the breakup of his empire there arose a mighty king named Chandragupta Maurya, who created an enormous empire along the Ganges River. His capital had the wonderful name Pataliputra. Chandragupta expanded his empire into the Punjab and then into Afghanistan where he fought a winning battle against the Greeks.

Chandragupta's grandson was Asoka, who some say was the greatest of all of India's kings. The Mauryan empire was enormous when this king ruled; it stretched from Bengal to beyond the Khyber Pass, and from the Himalayas south beyond the great river Kistna. Asoka was a just man, proud of his empire but also troubled by the cost of maintaining it, a cost not in money but in human suffering. He turned to Buddhism and through its teachings became one of the very few monarchs in history who forgave rather than punished. All over the empire he erected pillars or monuments on which he inscribed not the boasting words of a successful conqueror but the compassionate thoughts of a recontrite and just Buddhist:

"When an unconquered country is conquered, people are killed, they die, or are made captive. That I find very pitiful and grievous . . . if a hundredth or a thousandth part of those who suffered . . . were to be killed, to die, or to be taken captive, it would be very grievous to me. If anyone does me wrong, it will be forgiven as far as it can be forgiven . . ."

History tells us that Asoka really did try to carry out what he preached. He cut down on animal sacrifices, he encouraged pilgrimages, and he tried to reduce the severe penalties placed on wrongdoers. He even set up special officials whose only

job was to promote good feeling among people. He made a
very deep impression upon India, but his empire collapsed
soon after his death as men set to work to compete for wealth
and power.

There was a need for strong control in India in the centuries
after Asoka, but this control was rarely realized. Instead, one
invader after another poured out of the passes along the northwest frontier, and there was no one to stop them. Even far south
in the peninsula of India a good distance from invaders, kingdoms rose and fell in their own struggle for power. Some of
these southern people, known as the Tamils, even invaded
Ceylon and caused that country endless trouble.

In all this long troubled period, which lasted over a thousand
years, a great deal happened of tremendous importance to
India which, unfortunately, we can barely mention here.

Greeks who lived in the mountainous country of Afghanistan
invaded India and set up kingdoms around the Khyber Pass
region and in the Punjab. Though these kingdoms didn't last
very long, they brought India some of the knowledge of the
West, especially in subjects like medicine and astronomy.
Some Greek rulers even became Buddhists. There is a wonderful old document, called the "Questions of Menander," which
describes a discussion between a Buddhist wiseman and a
Greek king. Another later king during this period was the
famous Gondophernes, who is said to have been host to Saint
Thomas thus helping to bring Christianity to India.

About the time Vesuvius erupted and buried the Roman
city of Pompeii under tons of ashes (79 A.D.) a tribe of central
Asian nomads, who had been driven all the way from the
borders of China, were ruling much of northern India under
their king Kanishka. These were the Kushans, who are particularly remembered for their encouragement of Buddhism.

During the Kushan period a famous school of art flourished. This is the Gandhara school, named after the area in northwest India where it had its greatest patronage, and was remarkable for combining Western and Eastern art, a feat that affected art styles all the way to Japan. At places like Taxsila, a famous old capital city in the Punjab, archaeologists have found Buddhas seated yoga fashion, but with their hair curled like a Grecian Apollo and fully dressed in Roman togas!

The Romans were very conscious of India's wealth, and merchants from the Roman Empire found their way by land and sea to her shores. Roman coins have been found all over India, and recently archaeologists discovered a fine Roman port on the Bay of Bengal. Spices, ivory, jewels, perfumes, dyed cloth, peacocks, elephants—India had much to offer, and many a Roman lady may have prized a carved trinket from the bazaars of the Ganges or the shores of Malabar and Coromandel, just as Western ladies do today.

Indians like to think of the mighty empire of the Guptas that came later as a kind of classical period when much that was good happened. This empire controlled most of the territory once ruled by Asoka and the capital, Pataliputra, was the same. It was a time of great prosperity when the arts flourished and some of India's greatest thinkers and writers were roving about. The greatest of India's poets and playwrights was Kalidasa, who ranks with the finest artists of the world. Just read a few of his lines and you will know why. Listen to the sound of battle:

> Like the thundered threat of the angry death-god
> A great crash broke the walls of the ears,
> A shattering sound, tearing the tops of the mountains,
> And wholly filling the belly of heaven.

The host of the foe was jostled together.
The great elephants stumbled, the horses fell,
And all the footmen clung together in fear,
As the earth trembled and the ocean rose to shake the mountains.

And, before the host of the foes of the gods,
Dogs lifted their muzzles to gaze on the sun,
Then, howling together with cries that rent the eardrums,
They wretchedly slunk away.

Or see the wonderful pictures he paints:

And the wind forever shaking the pines
Carries the spray from the torrent of the young Ganges
And refreshes the hunting hillman,
blowing among his peacock plumes.

Or the lament of the husband separated from his wife:

I see your body in the sinuous creeper, your gaze in the startled
eyes of deer,
Your cheek in the moon, your hair in the plumage of peacocks
And in the tiny ripples of the river I see your sidelong glances
But alas, my dearest, nowhere do I find your whole likeness.

Kalidasa was also a master of drama and gave a tremendous
impetus to theater writing. Indian theatrical performances did
not take place in a theater but were and still are usually put
on in a courtyard of a house or temple by a group of pro-
fessionals. The drama was exactly like the dance in its depend-
ence upon gestures and body movement as the principal means
of expression. For every emotion or degree of emotion or
mood, there is a correct position for head, neck, eyes, hands,
feet, and body; and Indian actors and dancers must know

each and every one. Years and years of training are necessary before one can become a true artist and professional.

Among the other arts architecture and painting achieved great beauty. From very early times Indian temples were in caves. Even later, when architects could build in any way they wished, many of them still clung to the cave as the proper place for a temple. Elaborately carved and impressively conceived, India's cave-temples, most of them Hindu, are among the wonders of the world. Ellora and Elephanta are splendid examples, but the most famous of all are those of Ajanta. Here in vivid colors, great artists painted the walls with scenes from the world of ancient India as they knew it. Lovely Buddhist angels, flowers, birds, and animals mingle with the figures of hermits, princes, servants, and graceful ladies of India. Here is a treasure trove of wonders fifteen hundred years old.

So renowned was the Gupta empire that from far-off China bands of Buddhist monks came to refresh their knowledge of the faith by visiting the fine monasteries and shrines that were everywhere in the empire. One of these monks, Fa-Hsien, mentions in his diary how organized and peaceful everything was.

Peaceful and enduring as the Gupta world might have seemed, in less than 150 years from its founding, it collapsed. The White Huns grabbed the northern areas, and the rest broke into the little quarreling kingdoms again.

One energetic Indian monarch named Harsha built a fine empire for a while, which he ruled firmly but justly. Harsha was not only an excellent king but a good playwright as well. He was a patron of the arts and took great interest in religious matters, both Buddhist and Hindu. Another Chinese pilgrim, Hsian Tsang, was a guest at Harsha's court and through his account we have learned much of the life of the time. We are very anxious to read such accounts, for Harsha's state was the last of the great ancient Indian empires. The petty, little quarreling states along the Ganges could never be a match for the mighty powers that were rising to the West as the sword of Mohammed began to carve a new world.

Though the old India was dying, it had contributed an enormous number of useful things to the world. For one thing, it had developed Sanskrit, the great language of India, which has served the poets and thinkers of India very well and helped to preserve the splendors of India's philosophies and literature. Already vast areas of Asia were acknowledging India's religions, art, and technology. Countries like Burma, Siam, Ceylon, Tibet, and Java received much of their culture from India, and of course China and Japan had adopted Buddhism even more eagerly perhaps than had India.

Did you know that chickens, rice, sugar cane, and cotton originated in ancient India as good things to use? Then, too, the game of chess originated in India, as did the gypsies. Surgery and medicine were practiced with great skill. Indian doctors were especially skilled at plastic surgery and were able to smooth scarred faces and replace lost noses and ears when European doctors thought such things impossible. Thus British doctors gained valuable knowledge in India. Chaulmoogra oil, a medicinal product of a native Indian tree, is still used in the treatment of leprosy, but its beneficent effects in alleviating this dread disease were known for centuries by Indian doctors.

Greatest of all contributions perhaps was the decimal system, which helped open the door to the higher mathematics which made possible our modern world. And if you think

India's thinkers and writers did not influence the thinkers and writers of the West, read this by Walt Whitman:

> Lo soul, the retrospect brought forward,
> The old, most populous, wealthiest of earth's lands,
> The streams of the Indus and the Ganges and their many affluents,
> (I my shores of America walking to-day behold, resuming all,)
> The tale of Alexander on his warlike marches suddenly dying,
> To the south the seas and the Bay of Bengal,
> The flowing literatures, tremendous epics, religions, castes,
> Old occult Brahma interminably far back, the tender and junior Buddha . . .
>
> —*Leaves of Grass*

Murder and Moghuls

In the year 632 A.D. Mohammed, founder of the religion of Islam, died in Arabia. In his lifetime of some sixty-odd years he had established one of the world's greatest religions and converted thousands of Arabs to it. Belief in one God, Allah, with himself as spokesman of God, was the basis of the new creed. His sayings and the rules of the faith were gathered into a holy book known as the Koran. A part of the Koran describes how glorious it was to die in the name of Mohammedanism. Convinced that the world around Arabia was filled with idolaters who must either be converted or destroyed, Mohammed's followers began to crusade in foreign lands.

After Mohammed's death the Arab armies rapidly conquered Syria, Egypt, and Mesopotamia. Soon North Africa and Spain fell to the Mohammedans while in the East other Arabs smashed the feeble Persian armies and moved across the Iranian Plateau to the gates of India. In those days, no matter how far they might have gone, the Arab leaders owed allegiance to a spiritual and political leader called a *caliph*. The courts of these caliphs were splendid places enriched by the loot of the vast Arab conquests. They were also centers of intrigues and treachery.

Treachery, in fact, marked the first invasion of India. Thus in the eighth century a young general, Mohammed Ben Kasim, led troops out of the arid highlands of Baluchistan down into the Indus valley and up into the southern Punjab. Only seventeen years old when he started, at twenty-one the young man was conqueror of vast territories which he held in the name of the caliph. He was tortured to death on his return to Bagdad as a reward for his services, his enemies at home having had him destroyed out of jealousy. This event was a kind of warning of things to come.

For the next three hundred years the Moslems paid little attention to India. Then invasions began. The small Hindu kingdoms were unable to unite their forces, and shameful accounts of treachery and betrayal among them have come down to us. Thus a Turkish slave-king, Mahmud, ruler of Ghazni in Afghanistan, found the door to India wide open. No less than seventeen times Mahmud raided and looted northern India, leaving a trail of desperate sorrow in his wake. Fortunately Mahmud made no real attempt to stay in India; perhaps only the climate could beat him! A century later another Afghan prince, Mohammed of Ghor, picked up the pieces of Mahmud's empire and attacked India again. This time the desperate Hindu monarchs did unite, but they still clung to old ideas of fighting with elephants and moving about according to music, in contrast to the energetic, efficient Moslem armies. The result was a disastrous defeat for the Hindus, who never again rallied their forces.

The new rulers created the Sultanate of Delhi which from then on was the center of Moslem rule in India. And a disgraceful time it was. Murder, torture, treachery, destroyed one ruler after another. Little of lasting value was accomplished by anyone. It was a favorite game of the new rulers to destroy Hindu temples and monasteries, to burn books they considered heathen, and to smash idols, the wholesale destruction of people following that, of course. Far from obeying the Koran, sons killed fathers, and fathers their sons, meanwhile enjoying incredible luxuries. The whole monstrous record was topped by Timur-i-lang, known to history as Tamerlane, who sacked Delhi in 1398. It is said that thousands upon thousands were slaughtered and their heads heaped up in pyramids outside the walls of the city.

In spite of this horrid tale of centuries of destruction, some good resulted in this invasion of the East from the West. A few Moslems studied Indian life and ideas, and certain it is that learned Hindus were curious about Western knowledge as well. The Arabs of that time were great students of ancient knowledge, and at places like Córdoba in Spain, Damascus, Cairo, Samarkand, and Shiraz, medicine, astronomy, and the fine arts flourished. Some of this learning came to India, and certainly much Indian learning went to the West. For example, the decimal system and the concept of zero were carried westward, probably by Arab scholars.

As a welcome relief from the terrors of those centuries there came upon the scene another conqueror, a descendant of Timur. But whereas Timur was a kind of monster, his descendent Babur, the first of the Great Moghuls, was every bit a feeling, understanding man. (The term *Moghul* is really another way of saying Mongol, though actually Babur's men were Turkish and not Mongolians.)

Babur's diary has come down to us, and it is one of the really precious documents from the past that we have. It tells in a very straightforward manner how as a young man Babur tried to win back Samarkand the Golden, city of his forefathers, from its Uzbeg conquerors. He had little success, so he came to Kabul, the modern capital of Afghanistan, which was Babur's capital, too, and where his tomb is today. In ruling his kingdom, Babur showed great firmness and at the same time mercy, which in those fierce days was a unique thing. Eventually Babur invaded India and with a force of less than thirty thousand men smashed the vast armies of the Sultans of Delhi at the famous battle of Panipat.

"By the grace and mercy of almighty God, this difficult

affair was made easy to us and that mighty army, in the space of half a day, was laid in the dust."

Babur was helped in his conquests by his Turkish artillery-men, and an amusing story is told about the captain of these gunners. Babur and his men could not get used to the oppressive heat of India, so much so, that many wanted to go back to the cool mountains from whence they had come. But Babur knew that if this was done, their conquests would disappear overnight. One way around this dilemma was to build a new city which would have fountains, cool pavilions, and great green parks. He moved the capital from Delhi to Agra, where he laid out the new city. One of the works completed was a fine palace with an excellent dome in its roof.

One day the captain of the artillery called Babur out into the parade ground to show him a new cannon he had designed. In those days no one really knew how to use gunpowder effectively, so there were lots of experiments. Apparently Babur's old cannons could only throw stone balls several hundred yards at most; the new cannon was designed to exceed this range a little. With great pride, the artilleryman applied a torch to the torch hole. There was a great roar and a mighty blast that knocked everyone down and covered them with dust. As they sat there watching in astonishment, the cannon ball sailed over a thousand yards and went right through the new dome on the palace, wrecking everything in sight, but fortunately hurting no one. Turning toward the hapless gunner and seeing his look of consternation at the unexpected power of his new gun and the havoc it had wrought, Babur burst into laughter. Other rulers would have had the man executed, but Babur saw humor in the situation. The picture of the great emperor and his men sitting on the ground, covered with dust and howling with glee at the embarrassment of one of their number, is worth remembering. For it is one reason why Babur held the love of his men and could conquer, whatever the odds.

The end of Babur's life was characteristic. The story goes that his beloved son Humayun lay dying and there appeared to be no possible way of saving him. A wise man told Babur that the boy could be saved if the most precious thing in the empire was sacrificed. Some thought he meant treasure, but Babur knew what had to be done. He prayed to God and then walked around his son's bed three times saying: "Oh, God, I sacrifice my life, the most precious thing with me, for the sake of the life of my son."

Humayun began to recover, but on that same day his father became ill and shortly after died. Humayun became the new emperor. Whatever the truth of the story, it illustrates the respect that people had for the first of the Moghuls.

Humayun's son was the great Akbar, who brought the empire to its greatest extent until it rivaled that of Asoka. A man of great vigor, Akbar attempted to bring about a strongly united India under his rule. But in spite of all his efforts, he did not succeed.

The hatred between Hindu and Moslem was very deep by now. The dashing warrior princes of Rajputana and those of the Mahratta areas of central India could never rest under Moslem rule; they were in continual revolt. The most southerly parts of India kept their independence and deepened the Hindu quality of their culture. Roads were very bad and communications difficult, and that fact as much as any other made it impossible to bring about any lasting reform. Yet Akbar tried and his efforts to bring law and order equally to Hindu and Moslem created his fame. It is interesting that in Akbar's time another great monarch was ruling England. She was Elizabeth Tudor, whose reign was laying the foundation for the greatest empire in all history.

The successors of Akbar—Jahangir, Shah Jahan, and Aurangzeb—were the last of the Great Moghuls. The stories of their reigns would fill many books. Of Nur Mahal, the lovely princess whose efforts saved the throne again and again, of the peacock throne where the emperors sat, of the Red Fort— symbol of Moghul power—of Sivaji, the patriotic Mahratta chief who became the flame of freedom for the Hindus. Most memorable of all is that of the love of Shah Jahan for his wife Mumtaz Mahal, who died in the third year of his reign. The mausoleum he erected over her body took the labor of twenty thousand workmen and millions of dollars. The result was the Taj Mahal, which some say is the most perfect building in the world.

But the years of Moghul splendor ended as the old pattern of murder and treachery set in. The Persian king Nadir Shah took advantage of the situation and sacked Delhi, stealing

away even the peacock throne. Nothing remained but a few pathetic puppet emperors. The titles of the Great Moghul emperors had been worthy ones: Babur the Tiger, Akbar the Just, Jahan the Magnificent. But their successors were given names like the Pleasure-Lover and the Owl. One of the very last of the Moghuls was simply "You old man you!" How the great had fallen!

But one thing to keep in mind was that the Moghuls had deserved their title of *Great* not only because they were mighty conquerors, but also because they were patrons of learning and of the arts. Schools of painting integrated the lovely quality of delicate lines and soft shading characteristic of Persia with the warm color and exotic backgrounds of India. Taking the mosque domes and minaret towers of the Mohammedan Near East, architects in India surrounded them with fountains, pools, and gardens, using white marble and alabaster as building materials.

The Moghuls ruled at a time of great commercial activity in Europe. The spices, silks, crafts, and other products of the East were in great demand. Columbus, Vasco da Gama, and Magellan sought the sea roads to India in every direction. Those who reached India were struck by the splendors of the Moghuls. Such wealth was not to be ignored by enterprising merchants. Europe was bound to come to India, an eventuality which was to change India in ways both good and bad.

Clerk and Queen, Patriot and Poet

On August 15, 1947 the British Union Jack descended from the masthead on the viceroy's palace at New Delhi, and the modern states of India and Pakistan came into being.

The British had come to India over three hundred years before when a Moghul emperor still ruled at his court in Agra. Intent on setting up trading stations in order to secure the riches of the East for their distant island home, the English merchants of the seventeenth and eighteenth centuries were enterprising and aggressive, but they did not come to India as conquerors, at least at first. Certainly the first British to settle in India had no idea what was to happen. They were traders of the East India Company who got concessions from Moghul governors to occupy little trading places along the coast. Other European countries had done the same thing. The Portuguese and the Dutch were there even before the English, and the French were soon to follow. Each nation set up its own ports: Goa was Portuguese, and the French were at Pondichéry and Chandernagor. The British East India Company constructed its trade around Madras, Calcutta, and Bombay. Each place became a flourishing port with many warehouses, factories, offices, and homes, and of course a fort to retire to in time of trouble. And there was a lot of trouble, especially from the

French, who were the great commercial rivals of England not only in India but in Europe and America.

At first the French, under an able leader named Dupleix, had things very much their own way; they got the support of local Indian rulers and with their own troops took over many British possessions, including Madras. But one of the most celebrated English leaders in history came onto the scene. Young Robert Clive was a mere clerk at the time of the fall of Madras, but he soon convinced his superiors of his fighting ability and he gradually rewon much that was lost. At last, at the battle of Plassey (1757) Clive and three thousand men defeated the army of the Nawab of Bengal and his French allies, whose forces numbered over sixty-three thousand men.

From that time on, England expanded its possessions in India, sometimes by keeping the local ruler on his throne even though it took the wealth of his kingdom, other times by annexing whole territories and placing them directly under English control. Up the Ganges to the Punjab, across the peninsula, taking over territories that not even the great emperors Asoka and Akbar had ruled. Once started, the building of the empire went faster and faster.

But it wasn't always easy. Desperate wars were fought with the Mahrattas, the warrior Hindus of western India; with the Sikhs, the full-bearded people of the Punjab; and with the Afghans. During the First Afghan War (1839-1842) a British army marched to Babur's old capital, Kabul, but out of the thousands who stayed there only a few hundred ever managed to return. Betrayed into surrendering their guns, the British were shot by the Afghans without mercy as they tried to escape across the snowy passes of the frontier.

But wars were not all. In those days, before the steamship and the Suez Canal, it took months to go from England to Calcutta or Bombay. Clive once spent fifteen months getting there, months during which he battled against pirates, escaped from shipwreck, and witnessed the sinking of an accompanying ship with everyone on board.

Disease took a horrible toll. Sir Charles Napier, the commander of Sind, sailed with his men and their families on the short trip from Bombay to Karachi. Cholera broke out and within the ten days' sailing time 118 soldiers out of 299 were dead, and this does not count the wives, children, and crew whose bodies were tossed overboard. Somewhat later in Karachi, cholera again struck and in four days in and around that city fifty-seven thousand were dead. Sir Charles's nephew John had a pretty little daughter who died in the plague. The night of her funeral when John sat down to eat his supper, he too felt ill, and in three hours he was dead. The next day John's wife gave birth to another daughter. The sorrow of that family and of so many, many other families belongs to the story of the empire, too.

Another thing that made the task of ruling so hard was the boredom of doing the same job: keeping accounts and filing ledgers, and repeating the same words day after day after day to natives who did not understand. Clerks and agents were frequently stationed in lonely posts far from their fellow countrymen and they had to hold these posts under any conditions—extreme heat, illness, famine—and hold them for years at a time. I mention famine because it was another of the awful terrors that beset men as India's population grew beyond its safe food supply. This problem of increasing population and uncertain food supply affects India today. Its population is second only to China's.

One might ask why people let themselves in for so much trouble. For many it was the fact that a job needed to be done; for others there was always the chance that in India a soldier could find glory, a young man adventure, and a merchant untold wealth. The East India Company men did indeed accumulate tremendous fortunes, and some of their fine homes in England can be seen today. They are treasure houses of art and fine furnishings.

The worst of it was that once the wealth of India was obtainable, men quarreled over it and tried to work out more ways of squeezing more from the Indian land. For example, factories to manufacture cloth were purposely not built in India, but instead the cotton was shipped to places like Manchester in England where the cloth was made and then shipped back to India to be sold to the natives at a fine profit. This not only ruined the wonderful hand-weaving crafts of India but having ruined them, there was no place for the craftsmen to find work. And so it went. Many wise and able Englishmen tried to stop such abuses, but they could really do very little.

At last the whole mess exploded! So many things were wrong, it could not help but happen. The worst of it was that most of the British rulers were too far from the Indian people. They did not understand them or even try to. "Indian customs were silly, the people backward, and the British were not only their superiors but their masters." This kind of thinking, of course, did not fit too well on such proud people as the Rajputs or the Sikhs. Fortunately, there were Englishmen like the Lawrence brothers John and Henry who tried to reach the people by learning their language and their customs and giving them rule which retained their self-respect as well as maintaining law and order. So in the Punjab and on the northwest, where some of India's finest soldiers live, the Lawrences and others like them were able to keep the people loyal. And it is well that they did. For in 1857 the Indian army revolted. Some say it was because the soldiers (sepoys) discovered that the cartridges issued to them by their British officers were coated with pig grease. (Pig grease, is regarded as unclean by Moslems and many Hindus.) It was the last straw!

Delhi was seized by the mutinous troops. They even put a surviving Moghul prince on the old throne. Europeans were massacred wherever they appeared. The entire British population at Cawnpore was wiped out. Miraculous escapes occurred. One old servant, loyal to a British family, put the children in a big cooking pot and floated them down the Ganges out of danger. Others disguised themselves and got away. At Lucknow the British managed to fortify the residency of the governor, and there under the leadership of Sir Henry Lawrence they held out against months of attacks while wounds and sickness took their toll of men, women, and children. The mutiny was generally restricted to North India along the Ganges, the seat of the old empires, but everywhere else Indians waited menacingly to see what would happen next.

In England the public was horrified and ashamed. Horrified by the massacres and at the same time ashamed at the causes of it all. In India the handful of British and the few loyal troops remaining didn't wait for reinforcements. In five months Delhi was retaken and the mutineers routed, but only after a terrible cost in lives. At last the desperate defenders at Lucknow were relieved. There is a story told that when the defenders were at their lowest, when no help seemed possible, they heard the far-off skirl of bagpipes playing "The Campbells Are Coming." They called on one another to listen as if it were a dream, but it wasn't, it was the relieving force headed by Her Majesty's Regiment of Highlanders!

For England this outbreak was the Mutiny, for many Indians it was the Struggle. British rule was made tighter. The East India Company was abolished, and the British government ruled directly through its viceroys, who took the place of the company's governors general. Twenty years later Queen Victoria was crowned Empress of India, and the empire looked more imperial than ever.

But in many ways it really wasn't. There was still much of the old snobbery, and many British refused to recognize Indians as more than ignorant servants, but times had changed. Railroads, roads, telegraph lines, schools, modern cities, the Suez Canal (finished in 1869): these things not only allowed the English to rule more efficiently, but they also gave Indians more opportunity to learn. It was cheaper to train an Indian to learn English and then to make him a clerk, than to bring clerks all the way from England. Once a young man learned English, there was no stopping him from reading English books on such subjects as law, government, engineering, and history. At his finger tips was the hard-won knowledge of the Western world; and England of all countries had given the world certain fundamentals of freedom and justice without which, for example, the United States could not have been. More and more young Indians seized these opportunities to learn, and British teachers encouraged them in it. In fact, British leaders in all kinds of activities began to use educated Indians in important posts.

Nor was the education all one-sided. A great many Englishmen realized that the trouble in the past was caused by lack of knowledge of Indian customs. Handbooks began to appear giving details on Indian life, and British officials were required to know these things. Officers and civilian officials had to pass service examinations in Urdu or Hindi, the basic languages of India. Not only that, but if they were to be stationed in a particular part of India, they had to know the local language as well.

The next ninety years of British rule were good ones generally in spite of difficulties arising from young India's urge for freedom, world wars, and the changing world. In many ways these were amazing years, for as it turned out, rarely more than thirty or forty thousand Englishmen were ruling millions of Indians and doing it without using gas ovens, firing squads, pyramids of skulls, or concentration camps. In fact, Englishmen could go almost anywhere without fear of the assassination which was often the fate of imperial rulers in the world. Unfortunately, outsiders have been conditioned for years to think of British rule as almost entirely bad. The fact that there was a good side seems hard to imagine. But Indians generally acknowledge that the British were good rulers.

How did they rule so well? The answer to that problem is also beyond the scope of this book. But for one thing, they gained the *respect* of the people. In 1949 I took a trip north along the Indus River with an Englishman. Very early one morning we were awakened by a crowd approaching from a neighboring village. Someone had stolen some oranges, and two parties were accusing one another. They came right to the porch of our bungalow, ignoring the Americans and their own local official. They wanted the Englishman to judge the matter, even though England had given up its rule months before. The Englishman pulled up a chair, placed his hat beside it, heard the case, and in the people's own language gave judgment. They went away satisfied, for they felt they had received impartial justice.

On another occasion, high in the hill country of the northwest frontier, I watched a circle of fierce Pathan warriors sit by the hour on their haunches waiting for something. At last one of them arose, and the group broke up. How astonished I was when one of them came over to me and in perfect English inquired as to my work. It was an English officer dressed exactly as his Pathan soldiers. It turned out that the little son of one of his men had just died and the grief-stricken father had waited to get control of himself before returning to his village. His friends waited with him to encourage him, and as a father to each soldier, as well as their commanding officer, my English friend also waited hour after hour, sitting exactly as they did.

A medical missionary, Alfred Pennell, served over twenty-five years in Waziristan, home of some of the most hardy warriors in India. In all that time he converted less than a thousand souls, but at his death over 100,000 people came to pay their respects.

The English had a code of honor which made a very deep impression in a land where loyalty and self-sacrifice are worshiped in legend and story. Battle records tell of the death of hundreds of young English officers whose death did not have to occur, except that they would not retreat until the last wounded man was saved. How that impressed the warrior Sikhs, Pathans, Gurkhas (the warlike villagers of Nepal), and Rajputs! The civil official in some remote corner of the land quietly represented justice and authority. Each person has his place. No mingling at dinner or allowing oneself to be anything else but Sahib (Sir) to the people. How beautifully this fitted with the caste system, where each has a place and a job. Justice, courage, understanding, authority, all neatly blending India and England.

But there was discontent none the less, and no wonder! Indian leaders raised in the colonial tradition and now trained in the ideas of the West could hardly have been content with English rule. No matter how just the English might be, they were still foreigners ruling Indians, and few Indians had any voice in the government whose laws and edicts they had to obey. Indian leaders longed for the day when they would have a real part in governing their own affairs.

British rule over India was a complicated affair. There were really two governments. The first government ruled over territories directly administered by British officials; the second government was that of the princes, or rajahs, each of whom ruled ancestral lands. Some of these princely states, like that of the Nawab of Hyderabad, were enormous and contained millions of people; others consisted of no more than a few square miles of forest or agricultural land. Each princely ruler had his British advisor, and all owed allegiance to the English Crown through the Imperial Delegate, the viceroy, whose capital was New Delhi (1911–1947). There were hundreds of princely states, and maps of India in those days looked like patchwork quilts.

Education, sanitation, and technical progress were more advanced in those territories directly under British rule than under the rajahs. In order to rule so vast an empire, the British kept many Indian officials in office and upheld landlords in their possessions. As a result, there were many abuses. Problems of taxation, civil law, caste, famine, and land reform continued to plague the British administration. In correcting these, they pleased some people and offended others. Gradually the expense of governing India cut down the amount of profit gained by having India as a colony. Many British began to understand that British rule would have to end sometime.

Much of this understanding came about because educated Indians, many of whom were graduates of English universities, were speaking in no uncertain terms of India's need for self rule. These Indians, while demanding self rule, did not at first advise leaving the empire, because they realized the beneficent side of belonging to a larger family of nations under the Crown; they wanted a gradual acquisition of self rule as the Indians learned its responsibilities. A pioneer among these Indians was Surendranath Banerjea, who foresaw the rise of a united India. "In the name then of a common country, let us all, Hindus, Musulmans, Christians, Parsees, members of the great Indian community, throw the pall of oblivion over jealousies and dissensions of bygone times and embracing one another in fraternal love and affection, live and work for the benefit of a beloved Fatherland. Under English auspices there is indeed a great future for India. I am confident of the great destinies that are in store for us."

But dreams of a united India were doomed to disappointment. The basic trouble was a growing dissension between the Moslems and the Hindus. The Hindus far outnumber the Moslems in the subcontinent, there being at least three Hindus to one Moslem. If a parliamentary form of government like England's were set up, the Moslems would be hard put to gain more than a quarter of the votes at election time. "A united India would really mean Hindus dominating Moslems, Parsees, and Christians," the Moslems argued. In spite of all that the leaders of both groups could do to reconcile these problems, the two drifted farther apart. Moslems were proud people: they had come to India as conquerors; their Islamic faith was a unifying force that made them one people who were not divided by caste, class, province, and tribe as were the Hindus. Not since the days of Mohammed had there been such a unifying revival. A great poet, Mahomed Iqbal (1873–

1938), played up this oneness in the faith of Mohammed.
Today, he is considered to be the National Poet of Pakistan.

> A common aim shared by the multitude
> Is unity which, when it is mature,
> Forms the Community; the many live
> Only by virtue of the single bond.
> The Muslim's unity from natural faith
> Derives, and this the Prophet taught us,
> So that we lit a lantern on truth's way.
> This pearl was fished from his unfathomed sea,
> And of his bounty we are one in soul.
> Let not this unity go from our hands,
> And we endure to all eternity.

The Congress Party was the voice for all India in the beginning, but the dissensions between Moslem and Hindu caused the Moslems to form another party called the Moslem League. Frequently the leaders of both parties were in consultation, but real unity never came about.

The struggle for self rule produced a magnificent group of leaders in India, and in India and Pakistan they are celebrated today for their courage and foresight. But several were so outstanding that they belong to the world and are truly part of India's legacy to the world.

The first of these was the poet-patriot Rabindranath Tagore. Born in Bengal, Tagore wrote poetry from the age of thirteen, and in 1912 he won the Nobel Prize for Literature, a truly remarkable recognition for Indian culture as a whole. Tagore loved mankind. He saw the answer to the world's troubles in a return to the spirit that motivated the world's religions, whatever they were. He, too, wanted a united India, an India that would provide an example to the world of free men living by their faith. In the tradition of Kalidasa he wrote as a master poet, but as one listens, one hears the familiar tones of the ideals of liberty which were part of India's legacy from the West:

Where the mind is without fear and the head is held high;
Where knowledge is free;
Where the world has not been broken up into fragments by
     narrow domestic walls;
Where words come out from the depth of truth;
Where tireless striving stretches its arms towards perfection;
Where the clear stream of reason has not lost its way into the
     dreary desert sand of dead habit;
Where the mind is led forward by thee into everwidening
     thought and action—
Into that heaven of freedom, my Father, let my country awake.

The second great figure is that of Mohammed Ali Jinnah, known to the people of Pakistan as the Qaid-i-Azam, "the supreme leader, father of the nation."

Jinnah was a lawyer, born in Karachi and educated in England. As an educated Indian, he had opportunities to understand the problems of India and of the Moslems in particular. In spite of continued pressure advocating separate states, Jinnah at first worked diligently for Moslem-Hindu unity, but at last he saw that there was no hope of bringing the Congress Party to a realization of Moslem ambitions. He became the great champion of Pakistan independence. His numerous abilities and clear thinking made him a natural leader, and in no time he was the spokesman for the more than 75 million Moslems of India. In other circumstances he might have been taken for a model of an English gentleman. In manners, dress, and general deportment he was impeccable. A man of strong will, he hated the lack of dignity with which so many of his people conducted themselves whenever power or wealth appeared. He repeatedly pointed out the need for people to reach high and fulfill their true capabilities. He knew that the Pakistan which he was helping to create was in a sense artificial. With Bengal (East Pakistan) on the east cut off from West Pakistan by India, much of West Pakistan an arid desert, and the bulk of industry and mining wealth in India, Pakistan had only its generally impoverished people to make the country a reality.

Strangely, the name *Pakistan* originated at Cambridge University when a student, Rahmat Ali, made up the name for the Moslem nation which by 1930 Moslem leaders were envisioning as rising on the soil of India. The heaviest Moslem populations were in Bengal, the Punjab, Sind, Baluchistan, and the Northwest Frontier Province, as well as in Kashmir. Rahmat Ali's word *Pakistan* is a term made out of the letters for these provinces: P for Punjab, A for Afghania (his name for the Northwest Frontier areas), K for Kashmir, S for Sind, and TAN for Baluchistan. It means altogether, "Land of the Pure." (Bengal, on the east, was a problem that Rahmat Ali did not face in coining the name.)

Many Pakistani who knew Jinnah well have written about his sleepless nights and anxiety-filled moments. Again and again he appealed, cajoled, inspired, and welded his people. "Train yourselves, equip yourselves for the task that lies before us. The final victory depends upon you and is within our grasp. You have performed wonders in the past . . . You are not lacking in the great qualities and virtues in comparison with the other nations. Only you have to be fully conscious of that fact and act with courage, faith, and unity."

At last, worn out by his efforts, he died scarcely two years after Pakistan came into being. The nation he had created and started on its way remembers him as Americans remember George Washington. His code, simply and forcefully stated, can be read in many a home in Pakistan today, and school children learn it early in life: "Character, courage, industry, and perseverance are the four pillars on which the whole edifice of human life can be built, and *failure* is a word unknown to me."

Most famous in the West of all these great modern leaders of India is the little man in the simple white robe who was, above all, instrumental in bringing about India's independence. Mohandas Gandhi had been to London for a law education; he had fought for the rights of Indians in South Africa; he was deeply steeped in the enduring traditions of India. He knew well the ceaseless toil of the farmer and the endless finger movement of the hand spinner, and the rich tradition of religious belief that sustained village India throughout the cycles of the seasons. He knew and practiced dharma. But he also knew of the Sermon on the Mount, of Ruskin, and Tolstoy, and the great thinkers of the West. He was at once a dreamer and a practical man, as sensitive and deep-feeling a man as ever lived. He became, is now, and probably will be as long as modern India shall last, its patron saint. In fact, his title *Mahatma* means "the great-soul."

Gandhi did not believe in the adage "fight fire with fire." Rather than meet violence with violence, Gandhi preferred not to resist except by suffering—with pity for those who caused his suffering. Gandhi taught his followers that it was better to suffer for India's sake than to take guns and fight for her. When the British passed laws that were against India's hope for self rule, Gandhi's people simply went to jail rather than obey those laws. If any of his followers resorted to vio-

lence, Gandhi took the blame on himself and by so doing shamed those who caused it. The British jailed Gandhi for his resistance, but their sense of justice was such that Gandhi's letters from prison were circulated and his voice remained unsilenced.

Gandhi's love for India went so far as to advocate using only Indian hand products or, in other words, those things which were made in Indian villages. Indian weaving, for example, which had suffered because of the cheap cloth imported from England, was revived by Gandhi in order to make the people less dependent, and to take more pride in their own labor. India, as the land of cotton and jute, could very well revive its own weaving, especially that of the villages. So popular was Gandhi in the villages, that with their support he became the true leader of the Congress Party. He, too, tried to reconcile Hindus and Moslems and was heartbroken that the task proved impossible. Again, he was the great champion of giving rights to the "untouchables," those who really were outside or lowest in the caste system. He made himself one with the lowliest in India. "So long as a man does not of his own free will put himself last among his fellow creatures, there is no salvation for him."

Gandhi disciplined his body so that he got along with a very meager diet and the fewest possessions. Like the Buddha, he frequently fasted. His fasts were often protests against his followers' continuance of actions opposed to his idea of what was right. Personal hardship meant nothing. "To attain to perfect purity, one has to become absolutely passion-free in thought, speech, and action; to rise above the opposing currents of love and hatred, attachment and repulsion. I know that I have not in me as yet that triple purity, in spite of constant, ceaseless striving for it."

With such men and with disciples like Liaquat Ali Khan—later Prime Minister of Pakistan—and Jawaharlal Nehru, the British Empire had to contend. At last, worn out by two major world wars and a depression, resigned to a course of action already determined a hundred years before, Great Britain acceded and independence was achieved. The official time was August 15, 1947.

Surely at that moment thousands upon thousands of ghosts must have stood at attention, for it was one of the most solemn and dramatic moments in all history. If we could have seen some of those ghosts, we certainly would have noticed a stoutish man in a three-cornered hat; he would be Robert Clive, who with a small army and high resolve overcame all odds to lay the foundations of empire two hundred years before. There would be other ghosts of men and women, whose careers we haven't the space to outline, but whose names are worth remembering and about whom you should read. The shy-looking man with the grief-lined face would be Warren Hastings, who began the blending of East and West that created the empire. The hawk-faced man is Arthur Wellesley, the Duke of Wellington, who on the arid plains of India learned how to beat Napoleon. The two distinguished-looking brothers are the great administrators the Lawrences—John, the governor of the Punjab, and Sir Harry, the hero of Lucknow. And there are men in the grand military uniforms of the nineteenth century: John Nicholson, the peerless soldier of modern history, Charles Napier, the Lion of Sind; and "Ridin' Robbie" Roberts of Kandahar. Thackeray, Matthew Arnold, Thomas Moore and, of course, Rudyard Kipling would not be dim shadows in the ranks of the spirits. But all around them are others, so many others: kilted Highlanders, bearded Sikhs, green-hatted Gurkhas, little clerks with ink on their hands, great missionaries surrounded by unconverted multitudes who still worship their "Friend," wives and children, rajahs, nawabs and nizams, viceroys and governors general, water carriers and sweepers, and on and on.

The rise of great men such as Nehru, Gandhi, and Jinnah in India and Pakistan took place in the orderly world of the British Empire. Their lives were devoted to obtaining freedom from the final invader who had come to the shores of the subcontinent. But when these patriots had at last won their nations, their people were heirs not only to vast lands and rich traditions but also to the wisdom and training of the West. This they well knew, and whereas in other lands the monuments and buildings of empire have been smashed into ruins, the statues of Queen Victoria still grace the cities of India.

When the British left, the partition of India moved millions of people across the frontiers. Moslem and Hindu were caught in an agonizing odyssey of wandering, seeking new homes. Many died in the midst of hunger and civil strife. Gradually, however, matters adjusted; and though grievances remain, the two states of India and Pakistan are growing with the rest of the world. Each has immense problems to solve. Enormous populations and uncertain food supply, limited machine technology, and illiteracy are but some of these. However, if rich tradition, long colorful history, and enduring patience mean anything, the new states of the subcontinent will rise to fine achievement.

Chronological Chart of India
and World Events

Books for Further Reading

Index

	INDIA	NEAR EAST AND ASIA
B.C.		
4000–3000	First farmers arrive at Indus valley, about 4000	City-state civilizations develop from farming settlements in Tigris-Euphrates valley (Sumeria) and Nile valley (Egypt), about 3500
3000–2000	Harappan culture flourishes (beginning of Indian civilization), about 2100–1300	Chinese civilization begins, about 1700
2000–1000	Beginning of rice cultivation in tropical Asia, about 1500 Aryans and others begin invading India, about 1200	
1000–500	Buddha, about 560-487	Confucius in China, 551–479
500–1	Alexander the Great conquers Near East; crosses Indus River, 326 Maurya Empire founded along Ganges, 322–185 Coronation of Asoka, 269 Buddhism established as state religion Territory includes nearly all modern India, Afghanistan, and Baluchistan	
	Successive foreign invasions; divided kingdoms Roman trade reaches India, about 50 B.C.	Unification of Chinese Empire: Great Wall built, 246–210 B.C.
A.D.		
1–500	Kushan period, 78–220	Roman Empire master of Mediterranean, including Egypt and Near East, 116
	Gupta Empire (classical period; great prosperity), 320–647	Eastern Roman Empire (Byzantium) founded at Constantinople, 330
	Chinese pilgrim Fa-Hsien visits court, 399–414	
	Kalidasa, about 460 Arts flourish; Ajanta cave paintings White Huns invade India from northwest	
500–600		First great advancement of Byzantine civilization
600–700	Gupta territory dwindles; Harsha rules area in north only (last of great ancient Indian empires), 606–647	
	Chinese pilgrim Hsian Tsang visits Harsha's court, 630–643	
		Beginning of Arab Empire, 632; Arabs conquer Persia, Egypt, North Africa, Spain
700–800	Arabs conquer Sind under Mohammed Ben Kasim, 712	
800–900		Golden Age of Arab Empire (Abbasid Dynasty), 750–1258
		Arab traders bridge East and West
900–1000		Arab rule in Spain at height
1000–1100	Mahmud of Ghazni raids northern India, 1001–1027	
		Crusades against Moslems in Holy Lands, 1096–1270
1100–1200	Mohammed of Ghor conquers northern India, 1186–1206	
1200–1300	Sultanate of Delhi (center of Moslem rule in India), 1206–1526	Genghis Khan conquers central Asia and China, 1206–1221; Mongols overthrow Arab Empire, 1258
		Ottoman Empire (Turks) founded, 1288
	Marco Polo visits southern India, 1288, 1293	
1300–1400	Tamerlane sacks northern India, 1398	Tamerlane ruler of Asia from Russia to Persian Gulf, 1369–1405

India and World Events

	EUROPE	WESTERN HEMISPHERE
B.C. 4000–3000		
3000–2000	Early Minoan Age in Crete	First farmers arrive at Guatemala, Chiapas, and Yucatán, about 2000
2000–1000	Northern invaders overthrow Mycenaean civilization, about 1100	
1000–500	Greek colonies in Africa and Asia, about 575	
500–1	Alexander the Great (336–323) spreads Greek civilization over known Western world to India	
	Roman Empire founded, 27 B.C.	
A.D. 1–500	Roman Empire at greatest extent, 116	
		Maya period of prosperity, 300–700
	Final division into Eastern Roman Empire (Byzantium) and Western Roman Empire (Rome), 395 Visigoths sack Rome, 410	
500–600	Beginning of modern Western European civilization	
600–700		
700–800	Charles Martel defeats Moslems at Tours, France, 732; stops Arab expansion into Europe	
800–900	Charlemagne crowned emperor of Holy Roman Empire at Rome, 800	
900–1000	Arab rule in Spain at height; Cordova greatest intellectual center in Europe	Eric the Red discovers Greenland, about 985
1000–1100	William the Conqueror invades England, 1066 Crusades against Moslems in Holy Lands, 1096–1270	Leif Ericson visits Vinland, about 1000
1100–1200		
1200–1300	Magna Charta in England, 1215	
1300–1400	Ottoman Turks invade Europe, 1389	

	INDIA	NEAR EAST AND ASIA
A.D. 1400–1500		Ottoman Turks conquer most of Asia (control Arabs, 1453–1923); block trade routes to Far East

1500–1600	Vasco da Gama reaches India, 1498
	Portuguese conquest of Goa, 1510:
	  Beginning of European commercial
	  interest in India
	Babur defeats Sultanate of Delhi at Panipat,
	  1526: Beginning of Moghul Empire
	  Reign of Humayun, 1530–1556
		Ottoman Turks control lands of SE Europe, W Asia, and N Africa

1600–1700	Reign of Akbar the Just, 1556–1605
	  Empire comprises all of northern India;
	  unsuccessful attempt to unite Mos-
	  lems and Hindus
	  Fostering of learning and the arts
	First charter of British East India Com-
	  pany, 1600–1858
	Reign of Jahangir, 1605–1627
	  British Embassy to Moghuls, 1615–1618;
	  commercial treaty made
	Reign of Shah Jahan, 1627–1658; Moghul
	  power at highest point
	  Taj Mahal built, 1632–1645
	Reign of Aurangzeb (last of the Great
	  Moghuls), 1658–1707
	  Wars with Mahratta under Prince Sivaji,
	  1664–1680: Weakening of Moghul rule
	  Bombay founded, about 1669
	  Calcutta founded, 1690
		Manchu Dynasty in China, 1644–1912

1700–1800	Growth of British control under governors-
	  general of East India Company, 1740–1857
	Clive wins Battle of Plassey, 1757: Begin-
	  ning of British Empire in India	

1800–1900	First railroad opened, 1853
	Indian army "Mutiny" against British, 1857
	Abolition of East India Company, 1858: British
	rule India directly through viceroys, 1858–1947
	   Suez Canal, 1869, opens shorter trade route to E Asia:
	   European empires established throughout Asia and Africa
	
	Indian National Congress founded, 1885	

1900–	Moslem League founded, 1906
	
	Gandhi's campaign of civil disobedience,
	  1929
	Moslem League for Pakistan, 1940
	Partition of India into Pakistan and Republic
	  of India (Bharat), 1947
		Chinese Revolution, 1911–1912; Manchu
		  Dynasty overthrown
		End of Turkish Empire in Near East, 1923;
		  independent Arab states created, 1930–1945
		
		State of Israel established, 1948

	EUROPE	WESTERN HEMISPHERE
A.D. 1400–1500	Renaissance	Rise of Aztec civilization
1500–1600	Invention of printing, 1439 Moors expelled from Spain: Beginning of Spanish explorations in New World Vasco da Gama reaches India, 1498 Portuguese conquer Goa, 1510: Beginning of European commercial interest in India	Columbus discovers America, 1492 Aztec and Inca civilizations at height
	Magellan voyages around the world, 1519–1522	
	Turkish expansion into Europe stopped at Vienna, 1529 Reign of Elizabeth I in England, 1558–1603 Defeat of Spanish Armada, 1588; England gains control of seas	Cortes conquers Mexico, 1519–1521: Pizarro conquers Peru, 1531–1535
1600–1700	First charter of British East India Company, 1600–1858: Beginning of British Empire Dutch East India Company, 1602–1798 French East India Company, 1664–1769	Pilgrims land at Plymouth, 1620
1700–1800	Beginning of Industrial Revolution British become dominant power in India after Clive's victory at Plassey, 1757 French Revolution, 1788–1799	American Revolution, 1775–1783 Declaration of Independence, 1776
1800–1900	Napoleon defeated at Waterloo, 1815 Suez Canal, 1869, opens shorter trade route to E Asia: European empires established throughout Asia and Africa Queen Victoria of England crowned Empress of India, 1877	Civil War in U. S., 1861–1865
1900–	World War I, 1914–1918	U. S. enters World War I, 1917
	World War II, 1939–1945	U. S. enters World War II, 1941
	UN created, 1942; establish headquarters in U. S., 1946	
	British relinquish control over India; partition into Pakistan and Republic of India (Bharat), 1947	

Books for Further Reading

Allan, John, Haig, Sir T. Wolseley, and Dodwell, H. H., *The Cambridge Shorter History of India*. Cambridge, Cambridge University Press, 1934.

Basham, A. L., *The Wonder That Was India*. New York, The Macmillan Company, 1954.

The Cambridge History of India, 6 vols. Cambridge, Cambridge University Press, 1922–1937.

de Bary, William T., Jr., and others, eds., *Sources of Indian Tradition*. Introduction to Oriental Civilizations. New York, Columbia University Press, 1958.

Fischer, Louis, *The Life of Mahatma Gandhi*. New York, Harper and Brothers, 1950.

Kipling, Rudyard, *Barrack-room Ballads*. London, Methuen & Co., 1913.

——, *The Jungle Books,* 2 vols. New York, Doubleday & Company, Inc., 1948.

——, *Kim*. New York, Modern Library, Inc., 1950.

Lewis, Oscar, *Village Life in Northern India*. Urbana, University of Illinois, 1958.

Minney, R. J., *Clive of India*. London, Jarrolds Publishers, Ltd., 1957.

Nivedita, Sister (M. E. Noble), *Cradle Tales of Hinduism*. London, Longmans, Green & Co., 1907.

——, and Coomaraswamy, Ananda K., *Myths of the Hindus and Buddhists*. New York, Henry Holt & Company, Inc., 1914.

Piggott, Stuart, *Prehistoric India to 1000 B.C.* Harmondsworth, England, Penguin Books, 1950.

Rawlinson, H. G., *The Land and People of India*. New York, The Macmillan Company, 1955.

Roberts, Field-Marshal, Lord (of Kandahar), *Forty-one Years in India*. New York, Longmans, Green & Co., Inc., 1898.

Rowland, Benjamin, *The Art and Architecture of India*. The Pelican History of Art. Baltimore, Penguin Books, 1953.

Smith, V. A., *The Oxford History of India,* 3rd. ed., Percival Spear, ed. New York, Oxford University Press, 1958.

Spate, O. H. K., *India and Pakistan*. New York, E. P. Dutton and Co., Inc., 1954.

Swarup, Shanti, *The Arts and Crafts of India and Pakistan*. Bombay, Taraporevala's Treasure House of Books, 1957.

Wheeler, Sir Mortimer, *Early India and Pakistan to Ashoka*. London, Thames and Hudson, Ltd., 1959.

Wiser, C. V., and Wiser, W., *Behind Mud Walls in India*. London, G. Allen & Unwin, Ltd., 1932.

Index

125

About the Author

WALTER A. FAIRSERVIS, JR., internationally known archaeologist and anthropologist, has traveled extensively in India and the Near and Far East. His recent excavation of ruins in the Indus Valley dating from 2000 B.C. has added a new dimension to the cultural history of prehistoric India.

Dr. Fairservis attended the University of Chicago, the University of Michigan, and Columbia University and received his Doctor's degree from Harvard University. Now Research Associate in the Department of Anthropology at the American Museum of Natural History, he has directed three archaeological expeditions in Pakistan and Afghanistan. A frequent contributor to scientific journals, Dr. Fairservis is the author of archaeological studies published by the museum and of *Origins of Oriental Civilization,* published in the Mentor Series of New American Library. *India* is his first book for young people.

Dr. Fairservis, his wife, the illustrator Jan Fairservis, and their three children live in Pleasantville, New York.

6 7 8 9 10 72 71 70